CLYDE CRUISING CLUB
Sailing Directions and Anchora

GW00635232

Outer Hebrides

Contents

Edward Mason, Editor, Clyde Cruising Club Sailing Directions

© 2005 (Revisions to August 2009)
Published by Clyde Cruising Club Publications Ltd.
Suite 101, The Pentagon Centre, 36 Washington St. Glasgow, G3 8AZ
Tel: 0141 2212774, Fax: 0141 2212775, Email: hazel@clyde.org, http://www.clyde.org
Printed by Print Centric Ltd. Milnthorpe, Cumbria, LA7 7AD Tel: 015395 64592

Cover Photograph - The Sea Channel entrance to the pool, Rodel, Harris, by Randal Coe

Preface

The Clyde Cruising Club has published Sailing Directions for the West Coast of Scotland for over 80 years. The Club's Directions now cover in six parts, the Firth of Clyde, North Channel, Solway Firth and Isle of Man, the whole of the West Coast with all off-shore islands from the Mull of Kintyre to Cape Wrath, and also the North and North East Coasts of Scotland, and the Orkney and Shetland Islands.

This fully revised and extended new 2005 Edition covering the Outer Hebrides is Part 4. It is based to a large extent on the Edition of 1988 written and compiled by Dempster McLure, a former Editor of the Club's Sailing Directions. Dempster's thoroughness in his research resulted in a pilotage book which has been of great value to yachtsmen exploring the immensely intricate and remarkable chain of islands from Barra Head to the Butt of Lewis. This new Edition with plans in full colour and photographs will, it is hoped, encourage many more sailors to explore the Outer Hebrides, and even venture to visit the St Kilda group of islands which was recognised as a World Heritage Site in 1987.

I have received much assistance in the compilation of this new Edition. I am very grateful to Captain Calum Macleod, Harbour Master for the Western Isles, Dr John Macleod of Lochmaddy, and Dr Bill Speirs of Stornoway for their continuing interest and support during the preparation of this volume. We have been especially fortunate in having the advice and the expertise of Jon Hallam who has provided us with the results of his recent surveys and for these we are most grateful. A portion of his work is reflected in the new plans in this book for Acairseid Mhor, Eriskay and Poll an Tighmhail at Rodel.

In addition to those I have mentioned we need to thank all past and present members of the Club and very many others who over the years have contributed to the information contained in this volume.

The Clyde Cruising Club is very appreciative of the financial support given by Caledonian MacBrayne Limited towards the publication of these Sailing Directions.

Arthur Houston March 2005
Editor

Since the 2007 reprint of the 2005 edition a new chart of the Sound of Harris, No 2802, was published on July 2008. It is based upon the recent aerial surveys and has insets covering Bays Loch and Leverburgh. Unlike chart 2642, which it replaces, it is conventionally aligned to the meridian and is 800mm x 1130mm (A0) in size. The new chart consolidates the many changes to the buoyage that have taken place over the past few years and is vital for the safe navigation of this rock-strewn area.

Edward Mason August 2009
Editor

Caution These Sailing Directions are based on observations made over many years, together with a study of original surveys and aerial photographs, and consultation with locals and people with specialist knowledge. However, some places are rarely visited, and a complete knowledge cannot be claimed for all anchorages and passages under all conditions. While every effort has been made to ensure their accuracy, the information contained in these Directions and all amendments which are made to them, is selective and does not include all known information for each and every location described. This applies to both the text and the plans in particular, which should not be used for navigation. The Sailing Directions are written for yachts of moderate draft, and are not intended for larger craft. They should only be used as an aid-to-navigation in conjunction with current Admiralty charts, pilots and official hydrographic data. Skippers should not place reliance on these Sailing Directions in preference to exercising their own judgement.

Disclaimer **Clyde Cruising Club Publications Ltd. and the Clyde Cruising Club (including its individual Members and specifically but not limited to those Members acting as editors and as authors) entirely exclude any and all responsibility or liability for any loss, injury, damage, expenses or costs incurred by any person whether directly or indirectly from any error in or omission from these Sailing Directions or any subsequent amendments.**

Note **The cut off date for the pilotage information in this re-print is 1st August 2009.** Future additions and amendments may be obtained from the Sailing Directions page, which is maintained by Clyde Cruising Club Publications Ltd, within the Club's website (http://www.clyde.org) or by writing to Clyde Cruising Club Publications Ltd. c/o the Club office.

Outer Hebrides

Introduction

Sailing in the Outer Hebrides

General
The east side of the Outer Hebrides which is sheltered from the prevailing westerly winds and the Atlantic Ocean has innumerable well sheltered anchorages. These anchorages, some large and some small, are often within a short distance of each other. Some are easily approached while others require great care and very skilful pilotage. From the islands S of Barra, to the Uists and Benbecula and then northwards to Harris and the Isle of Lewis, the east side of the Hebrides forms an extended chain of islands, inlets and islets, which provides a rich source of intriguingly different anchorages, many of which are remote from habitation.

Approaching the Outer Hebrides from the E it is better to make initially for one of the centres of population e.g. Castlebay (Barra), Lochboisdale (South Uist), East Loch Tarbert (Harris), or Stornoway (Lewis). Whilst Loch Skipport, South Uist in the S, and Loch Shell, Lewis in the N are relatively easy to identify and enter, and provide well sheltered anchorages, neither has any facilities. Initially it is better to explore the more isolated lochs and difficult entrances from one of the foregoing locations. It would be dangerous to approach unfamiliar landfalls in poor visibility with the obvious difficulty of identification. Similarly night sailing cannot be encouraged until the visitor is familiar with the area and even then the additional risks may best be avoided. However, such risks could be minimised with the aid of GPS (with appropriate correction to comply with WGS 84 datum) where applicable.

From the S, the west side of the Outer Hebrides has little shelter until the Monach Islands are reached. However from here northwards, well sheltered summer anchorages can be found in the areas of West Loch Tarbert, Loch Resort and Loch Roag. Being exposed to the open Atlantic these lochs are best visited in settled weather with an experienced crew. Many places are remote from habitation but with VHF wireless communication links with Stornoway Coastguard, weather information and assistance, if necessary, is available.

Some anchorages are more easily approached near low water when some of the dangers are visible. The advantages of a rising tide are obvious.

A reliable echo-sounder is often an essential aid to pilotage. A 'safe depth' to clear hazards may usually be found from the chart, but this may be over 30m, and the instrument must be capable of giving readings at twice the depth selected.

In many anchorages the bottom is mud, sometimes too soft to provide good holding, but in general it is mostly satisfactory. Weed is frequently found, and choice of ground tackle must take this into account. It is worth taking care to avoid putting the anchor down on weed. Rock is usually confined to odd patches, and many anchorages, usually within the sounds between the main islands, have clean white sand. Some of the most apparently sheltered anchorages are subject to severe squalls off surrounding hills, especially in steep-sided lochs.

Fishermens' floats and stray lines may be encountered up to 12 miles offshore especially out W. The same risk exists in conditions of fast tidal flow off headlands. In either case it could be hazardous to become entangled with them. Often they are partially submerged and difficult to see and a sharp lookout is required at all times.

Fish farming equipment has increasingly been established in many inlets in the Outer Hebrides, especially in Harris and Lewis. They are not usually lit and a good lookout should be kept if attempting to enter an anchorage in the dark or in conditions of poor visibility.

Tidal streams
The general direction of tidal streams around the Outer Hebrides is N-going (in-going, flood tide) and S-going (out-going ebb tide). However the in-coming tide runs E at the Butt of Lewis and S to meet the N-going stream off the entrance to Stornoway. The in-coming tide runs E in the sounds S of Barra but enters the Sound of Barra from both ends. In the Sound of Harris the tides are complex but can usually be predicted at the various parts of the Sound.

Weather
Westerly winds predominate at Castlebay and S-SW at Stornoway, where NE winds are most common in May, and fairly common in April and June. Rainfall is lowest in May and June, and in the Southern islands is generally less than the mainland. Gales occur on average on less than half a day per month at Castlebay during April-September, one day per month at Stornoway during May-August, but three days in March and September. Visibility of less than half a mile may occur on three days per month in mid-summer, but usually the frequency is much less. Visibility of less than two miles does not normally occur on more than three days per month.

Forecasts
As this area is normally on the windward side of the country, weather forecasting may seem less reliable than elsewhere. Usually this is a matter of timing than of general synopsis, coupled with the fact that Shipping Forecasts are for Sea Areas extending well out into the Atlantic. The weather inshore is likely to be greatly affected by the configuration of the land.

Introduction

Sailing in the Outer Hebrides (continued)

Local forecasts

Inshore Waters Forecasts
BBC Radio 4 198 kHz (1500m) after Shipping Forecasts at 0048 and 0535.

Shipping Forecasts
BBC Radio 4 198 kHz (1500m) - Sea areas Malin and Hebrides at 0048, 0535, 1201 and 1754.

Landward Forecasts
BBC Radio Scotland 810 kHz (370)

Coastguard Forecasts
In addition to the BBC Shipping and Inshore Waters forecasts, local forecasts for the area from **Ardnamurchan to Cape Wrath** are forecast by **Stornoway Coastguard.** The area is divided into two: 1. Ardnamurchan Point to Cape Wrath, excluding the Minch, and extending up to 12 miles W of the Outer Hebrides and 2. The Minch, bounded by lines from South Uist to Rum in the South, and the Butt of Lewis to Lochinver in the North. Initial announcements are made on ch. 16 and thereafter the forecasts are made from the following aerials; Arisaig ch. 23, Sound of Sleat ch. 86, Portree ch. 84, Melvaig (Loch Ewe) ch. 23, Stornoway ch. 84 and Butt of Lewis ch. 86. Listen for the strongest signal on these channels for optimum reception. Forecasts by Coastguards are made at **local time**, i.e. the 'clock time' that the broadcast is made remains the same throughout the year. The forecasts by Stornoway Coastguard are made every three hours commencing at 0110 and thereafter at 0410, 0710, 1010, 1310, 1610, 1910, and 2210. In addition **Clyde Coastguard** also broadcasts forecasts for Area 2, every three hours commencing at 0210 and thereafter at 0510, 0810, 1110, 1410, 1710, 2010, and 2310. The times given are not precise as forecasts may be delayed or omitted during casualty working.

Lights
The Minch and Sea of the Hebrides are reasonably well lit, being used by commercial traffic. Loch Boisdale, Loch Carnan, Loch Maddy, Cope Passage (Sound of Harris), Castlebay, East Loch Tarbert (Harris) and Stornoway (Lewis) are well enough lit to be approached at night in moderate conditions. On the W side of the Outer Hebrides only East Loch Roag (Lewis) is lit to allow an approach at night. For passage making on the W side of the Hebrides there are lights on the Flannan and Monach Isles.

Equipment
It is essential that any yacht cruising in the Outer Hebrides be well found and well equipped. Standards laid down in the Royal Yachting Association's publication C8 "Boat Safety Handbook" provides sound standards to follow and is obtainable from www.rya.org.uk/shop, price £5.50.

Anchors
It is essential to have at least two anchors of not less than the weight recommended by the anchor manufacturers for the size of the boat, with appropriate size of cable. These weights are likely to be greater than those supplied by manufacturers of stock boats. At least 60m of chain should be available so as to be able to let out at least four times as much chain as the depth at high water. An "angel" or weight to let down the cable to reduce snubbing in heavy conditions is always worth carrying. In view of the variety of conditions two different types of anchor should be carried. The choice is very much a matter of individual preference, but the Bruce and CQR types seem less likely to pick up weed than the Danforth Meon type. Where the water is clear it is worth going to considerable trouble to drop the anchor clear of boulders and weed. Tripping lines should certainly be used in the vicinity of fish farms. When cages are moved often old moorings remain. Swinging room must be left for any vessel already anchored, including allowing for changes in wind direction.

Anchorages & moorings
Under suitable conditions adventurous yachtsmen will find, with the help of charts and sketch plans, anchorages other than those described in these Sailing Directions. **Visitors moorings** for vessels up to 15 tons maximum are available at Castlebay, Acairseid Mhor (Eriskay), Loch Boisdale, Loch Maddy, and Rodel (Harris). Charges are now levied for moorings and Council owned piers. Contact the Council HM on 01870 602425 to arrange for payment.

Piers & Jetties
May be used by fishing boats, ferries or other vessels, and yachts should never be left unattended alongside without it being made absolutely certain that access will not be needed. Stornoway is the only location where there are marina pontoon berths although loading pontoons may be found at fishing centres.

Fish Farms
Fish farm cages of many types can be found anywhere within suitable mooring depths in sheltered waters. These are numerous and their locations are constantly changed. The extent of their moorings is generally marked by yellow buoys but, as these are not always lit, a good lookout must be kept when entering an anchorage or harbour at night or in poor visibility. Anchor well clear of any such buoys. Tripping lines are strongly advised.

Cables
Submarine power and telephone cables have been laid across many lochs and channels and their presence is indicated by shore marker boards with a red diamond on a RW post. The North of Scotland Hydro Electric Board urges yachtsmen to avoid anchoring anywhere near cables and to remember that they do not necessarily lie in a straight line on the sea bed between markers.

Introduction

Sailing in the Outer Hebrides (continued)

Diesel Marine diesel is available by hose at only the following locations: Brevig (Broad Bay), Stornoway, Carloway, Kirkibost, Miavaig, Scalpay, Stockinish, Leverburgh, Berneray (North Uist), Griminish, Kallin, Ludag (Sound of Eriskay - West), Eriskay (Acarseid Mhor), Vatersay (causeway slipway) and North Bay, Barra. All installations apart from North Bay (which is suitable for large quantities only) are operated by the Western Isles Council. The system is unmanned and requires users to have a key card. These can be obtained **on prior application to the Council** and a few days must be allowed for the issue of the card. Application should be made to: The Harbour Master, Comhairle nan Eilean Siar, Balivanich, Isle of Benbecula. HS7 5LA. Tel: 01851 703773. It is also possible that in 2010 users may be able to obtain a card directly from an agent in Stornoway. Card holders are required to register as leisure or commercial users and will be invoiced monthly at the appropriate duty and VAT inclusive rate.

Emergencies

Coastguard HM Coastguard Service is responsible for initiating and coordinating all civil maritime search and rescue measures for vessels or persons in need of assistance in the United Kingdom Search and Rescue Region. The Service maintains a continuous listening watch on VHF Ch16, and operates a safety service on Ch 67. The Clyde Maritime Rescue Coordination Centre (MRCC) the Maritime Rescue Sub-centre at Greenock (tel: 01475 729988) along with the Maritime Rescue Sub-centre (MRSC) at Stornoway (tel: 01851 702013) are responsible for rescue matters in the area covered by these Sailing Directions.

Lifeboats All-weather lifeboats are stationed at Stornoway and Castlebay.

Communications

Sea Oban to Castlebay, Barra and Lochboisdale, South Uist
Uig, Skye to Lochmaddy, North Uist and East loch Tarbert, Harris
Ullapool to Stornoway
Leverburgh, Harris to Berneray and North Uist across the Sound of Harris
Eriskay to Barra across the Sound of Barra
All the foregoing are operated by Caledonian MacBrayne (tel: 01475 650100)

Air Glasgow, Edinburgh, Inverness to Stornoway
Glasgow to Barra and Benbecula
For details of operators contact Western Isles Tourist Board. (Tel. 01851 703088)

Notes on Sailing Directions and Plans

Bearings The bearings given in these Sailing Directions both in the text and on the plans are always from seaward and always refer to True North. All plans are orientated with True North at the top as the plan is read. Note that certain of the longer transits given in these directions may not be readily identified.

Depths & heights All Depths and Heights in the text are in Metres. Depths are in metres below Lowest Astronomical Tide (LAT). This datum (Chart Datum) is the lowest level to which the surface of the sea will fall due to astronomical causes. High barometric pressure or strong offshore winds combined with a low spring tide can cause the level to fall lower. Drying heights of rocks are related to Chart Datum. Heights on land and above-water rocks and bridges and cable clearances are related to MHWS.

These directions are primarily written for yachts of moderate draft, of 2 metres or less. Shoal draft yachts will find many more anchorages and passages available to them.

Some anchorages and passages are only suitable for very manoeuvrable yachts in the hands of crews familiar with local conditions. All information available should be carefully consulted, and the scale of charts and plans must be appreciated before making an approach. Some anchorages are more easily approached near low water when some of the hazards may be visible. Some places are remote from habitation, and assistance may be hard to come by.

Even with a reliable echo-sounder some dangers project so abruptly from the bottom as to give no warning by observing the depth, but usually the depth will be a valuable guide, as may be found from a study of charts and plans.

Introduction

Notes on Sailing Directions and Plans (continued)

Tide Constants are given for both Ullapool and Dover. The use of Ullapool will give greater accuracy. Note that constants are for rise and fall of tides, not for change of direction of tidal streams. The spring range is between 3.4 metres in the islands south of Barra to 4.2 metres in Harris and Lewis.

Place names In some cases the popular name for a place, or its spelling, differs from that on Admiralty Charts. The latter is usually given, and both where appropriate.

Marks Only those used in identifying and approaching the entrance to an anchorage, or for coastal passage-making, are listed separately. Inner marks are referred to in the approach directions to anchorages and harbours.

Lights Light characteristics are as used on Admiralty Charts and a key to the abbreviations will be found inside the front cover.

Charts It is emphasised that sufficient Admiralty Charts must be carried. Below is a full list of charts for the area covered by these Directions, grouped according to their scale, and listed from South to North.

Group (i) Charts covering the whole area and which are useful for cruise planning and navigation in open water

Group (ii) Complete coverage of the charts listed at the scales of 1:100.000 and 1:50,000 should be carried as appropriate for the the extent of the cruise which is contemplated.

Group (iii) Charts at a scale of 1:30,000 or larger. Some of these are essential to the extent that it would be hazardous for a stranger to enter the waters covered without the appropriate chart. Those charts which are considered essential for safe navigation in certain areas are indicated with an asterisk (*). Even in other areas it may be found that a yacht is confined to a main fairway by not having a chart at the largest scale available.

Charts & Publications

	Number	Title	Scale	Includes
Group (i)	2635	Scotland, West Coast	500,00	
	2722	Skerryvore to St Kilda	200,000	Barra Head to N Uist and Sound of Harris
	2721	St Kilda to Butt of Lewis	200,000	N Uist, Flannan Isles
	2720	Flannan Isles to Sule Skerry	200,000	Butt of Lewis, Ru Stoer, Cape Wrath, Rona and Sule Sgeir
Group (ii)	1796	Barra Head to Point of Ardnamurchan	100,000	Barra, Canna, Rhum, Coll, Tiree
	1795	The Little Minch	100,000	E Coast of S Uist, Benbecula, N. Uist, Sound of Harris, W Coast of Skye, Rhum, Canna
	1794	North Minch - Southern Part	100,000	E Loch Tarbert (Harris), Stornoway, Ru Stoer, Lochinver, Loch Ewe, Loch Gairloch
	1785	North Minch - Northern Part	100,000	Stornoway, Butt of Lewis, Cape Wrath, Kinlochbervie, Ru Stoer, Lochinver
	2841	Loch Maddy to Loch Resort incl. Sound of Harris	50,000	North Uist to Loch Resort
Group (iii)	*2769	Barra Head to Greian Head	30,000	
		Castle Bay	12,500	
	*2770	Sound of Barra	30,000	
		Loch Boisdale	12,500	
	*2904	Usinish to Eigneig Mhor	25,000	
	2825	Lochs on E Coast of Uist		
		Loch Skipport, Loch Carnan, Loch Maddy	12,500	
		Loch Eynort, Loch Eport	15,000	
	*2802	Sound of Harris	21,000	
	2905	East Loch Tarbert	12,500	
	2529	Approaches to Stornoway	25,000	
		Stornoway Harbour	10,000	
	*2515	Ard More Mangersta to Tiumpan Head including Loch Roag	25,000	
	2524	Islands of the North West Coast of Scotland	various	St Kilda, Flannan Islands, Sule Sgeir and Rona

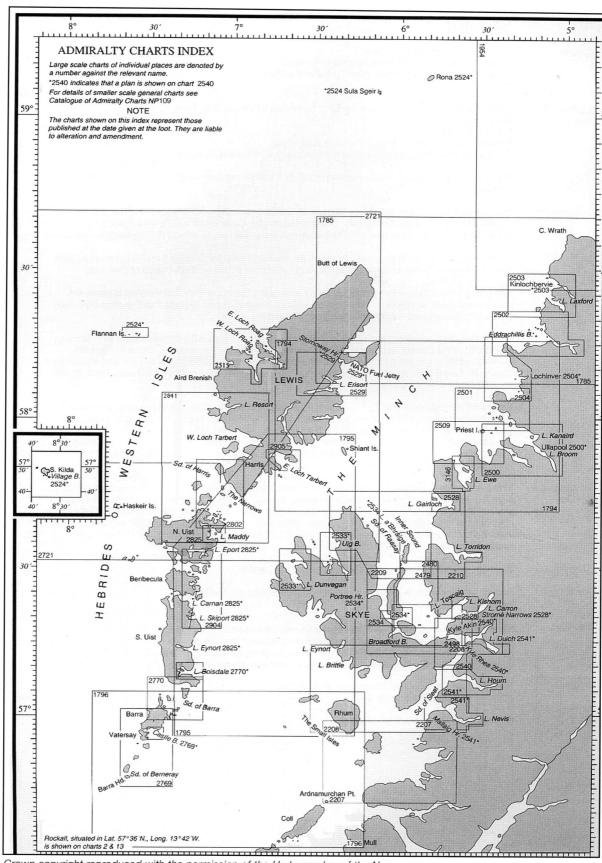

Introduction

Charts & Publications (continued)

References **Admiralty Publications**
Admiralty West Coast of Scotland Pilot, 14th Edition 2001 (NP 66)
Admiralty Tidal Stream Atlas (NP 218) N Coast of Ireland and West Coast of Scotland
Admiralty Tide Tables Volume 1 (NP 201)
Admiralty List of Lights Volume A (NP 74) British Isles and N Coast of France
Admiralty Supplements for Sailing Directions (NP 66) and Notices to Mariners

Almanacs
Reeds OKI Nautical Almanac (Western Edition)
Reeds PBO Small Craft Almanac

Admiralty Chart Agents
Glasgow Kelvin Hughes Tel. 0141 221 5452
Aberdeen Thomas Gunn Navigational Services Tel. 01224 595045

Chart Distribution in West Scotland

| Mallaig | Johnston Brothers | Tel. 01687 462215 |
| Oban | Nancy Black | Tel. 01631 562550 |

Ordnance Survey Maps for the Outer Hebrides
These maps at a scale of 1: 50,000 are extremely useful as they provide topographical detail which has
been omitted from the plans in these directions and supplement the detail shown on the Admiralty Charts.
The Landranger Series which are relevant comprise:
31 Barra, Eriskay and South Uist
22 South Uist and Benbecula
18 North Uist and Sound of Harris
14 South Harris
13 West Harris and Lewis
8 Stornoway and North Lewis

Bibliography The Yachtsman's Pilot to the Western Isles by Martin Lawrence published by Imrays, 2003.
Islands of Western Scotland : The Inner and Outer Hebrides by W.H.Murray published by Eyre Methuen
The Scottish Islands by Hamish Haswell-Smith published by Canongate, Edinburgh
David and Charles' Island Series : Uist and Barra, Harris and Lewis, St Kilda and Hebridean Outliers
Harris and Lewis (Outer Hebrides) by Francis Thompson published by David and Charles ISBN 0 7153
   8934 3)
Discovering Lewis and Harris by James Shaw Grant published by John Donald Publishers Ltd, Edinburgh
ISBN 0 85976 185 1
Innsegall, the Western Isles by Barber and Magee published by John Donald Publishers Ltd, Edinburgh
ISBN 0 85976 142 8
The Highlands and Islands by F. Fraser Darling and J. Morton Boyd published by Collins, 1971
Crofting Years by Francis Thompson published by Luath Press Ltd ISBN 0 946487 065
A Hebridean Naturalist by W.A.J.Cunningham
Birds of the Outer Hebrides by Peter Cunningham published by Melven Press ISBN 0906 64 00
Scottish Mountaineering Club Guide : Islands of Scotland
The Age of Stonehenge by Colin Burgess published J.M.Dent, 1980
Guide to Prehistoric Scotland by Richard Feachan published by Batsford Ltd, ISBN 0 7705 1475 8
Exploring Scotland's Heritage, Argyll and the Western Isles published HMSO ISBN 0 11 492429 5

Passage making to the Outer Hebrides

Charts
1796	Barra Head to Point of Ardnamurchan
1795	The Little Minch
1794	North Minch - Southern Part

General There are three distinct sea areas to be considered when contemplating crossing to the Outer Hebrides. From
South to North these comprise:- (a) the Sea of the Hebrides between the mainland of Scotland in the vicinity of the
Point of Ardnamurchan to Barra and northwards to Loch Skipport in South Uist (see p. 10), (b) the Little Minch
between Skye, North Uist and Harris (see p. 76), and (c) the North Minch between the mainland from Gairloch in
the South to Lochinver in the North across to Lewis (see p. 85)

Introduction

Evening ferry leaving Castle Bay with Vatersay Bay beyond   *Charles Tait*

Sunset over Pabay Mor and Vacsay, West Loch Roag   *Pat and Jill Barron*

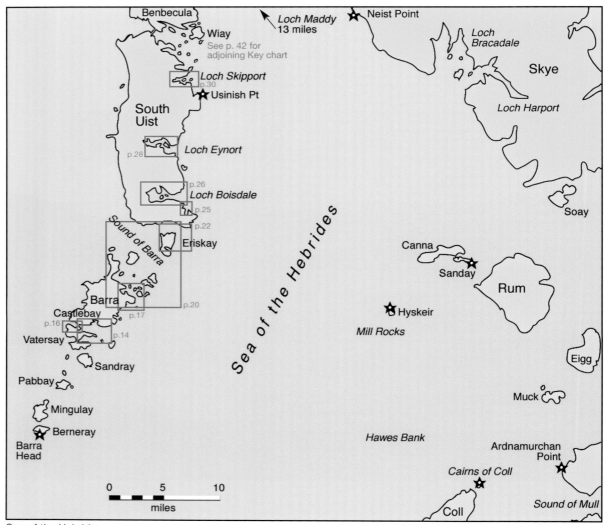

Sea of the Hebrides

Crossing the Sea of the Hebrides

Charts
1796   Barra Head to Point of Ardnamurchan
1795   The Little Minch

Lights

Ardnamurchan LH	Fl.(2) 20s 55m 24M Vis 002°-217°	Grey granite Twr
Cairns of Coll	Fl.12s 23m 10m	Wh twr
Hyskeir (Oigh Sgeir) LH	Fl.(3) 30s 41m 24M (Racon 'T')	Wh Twr 5M SW of Canna
Sanday (Canna)	Fl.10s 32m 9M	Wh. Twr.
Barra Head LH	Fl.15s 208m 18M	Wh. stone Twr
Ushenish, South Uist	Fl.WR 20s 54m W19M R15M	Wh. Twr
Neist Point, Skye	Fl.5s 43m 16M	Wh. Twr.

Distances
Sound of Mull to Castlebay, Barra 50 miles
Sound of Mull to Canna 25 miles
Canna to Castlebay, Barra 35 miles
Canna to Eriskay 26 miles
Canna to Lochboisdale 25 miles
Canna to Loch Skipport, South Uist 30 miles
Canna to Loch Maddy, North Uist 40 miles

Tides
These are generally weak offshore. Sea conditions are more likely to be affected by cross seas following a period of unsettled weather.

Crossing the Sea of the Hebrides (continued)

General   The significant hazards in the Sea of the Hebrides are the Cairns of Coll, the potential for breaking seas on the Hawes Bank W of the Cairns of Coll (minimum depth 16m), the Mill Rocks S of Hyskeir, and the identification of landfalls in conditions of poor visibility. This is particularly the case in the approach to Castlebay. The convenience of **Canna Harbour** as a jumping off point for passage across the Sea of the Hebrides and northwards towards the the Little Minch for a landfall on North Uist cannot be overemphasised. Distances and weather conditions make Canna the most favoured anchorage for departure and return. (See passage description p. 25)

Landfalls   For **Castlebay**, Barra, Heaval (382m), the highest hill on Barra, and Muldoanich Island (151m) one mile E of Vatersay, are prominent, together with the Bo Vich Cuan S card. buoy Q(6) + LFl.15s which gives warning of dangers in the approach.

For the identification of **Eriskay** is best understood with reference to the hills S of Loch Boisdale. The appearance of these hills, along with the two groups of mountains N of Loch Boisdale, during the outward passage is described on pp. 24 & 25 which deal in detail with approaches to the East side of South Uist.

For making landfalls at **Loch Boisdale** and **Loch Skipport** see the descriptions given on pp. 27 & 31.

The SE approach to **Loch Maddy**, North Uist, is significantly assisted by by the dominant feature of Eaval (345m) a wedge shaped mountain at the southern extremity of North Uist.

Islands to the South of Barra

Charts   (ii) 1796   Barra Head to Point of Ardnamurchan
(iii) 2769   Barra Head to Greian Head
OS 31

General   Of these islands to the south of Barra only Vatersay is inhabited, offering, in Vatersay Bay, anchorage sheltered from all winds and free from swell at its head. The other islands, Sandray, Pabbay, Mingulay and Berneray provide, in settled conditions, some limited anchorage and shelter from wind and swell. Nonetheless, these southern islands with surrounding islets and sounds present a fascinating blend of land and sea with their birdlife and spectacular views of cliffs within a comparatively short distance of secure anchorages in Barra or Vatersay Bay.

Tides   Const. —0108 Ullapool (—0528 Dover) MHWS 4.0   MHWN 3.0   ML 2.4   MLWN 2.4   MLWS 0.8
From the E side of Berneray in the S to East Loch Tarbert, Harris, in the N, the tidal flow closer in to the E coast differs greatly to those in the Sea of the Hebrides. Three to four miles E of the coast those in-shore tidal currents change to those more normal to the Sea of the Hebrides. (See Admiralty Tidal Atlas NP 218.) On the E side near the coast from Berneray to the Sound of Barra the streams begin two hours earlier than off Barra Head and run in the general direction of the coast as follows:

NE-going stream begins +0520 Ullapool (+0100 Dover)
SW-going stream begins —0400 Ullapool (—0500 Dover)
The spring rate in each direction is 1.5 kn off headlands and entrance to bays. In the bays and further to seaward the rate is less. In the sounds between the islands rates increase up to 3kn at springs.

Light   Barra Head Lt. Ho. (on Berneray) Fl 15s 208m 18M Wh. Twr

Caution   In most winds, even in moderate E winds, the sea state on the E side of the islands is relatively quiet. However dangerous breaking seas can occur at the E entrances to the sounds between the islands in strong E winds against tide. Similarly on the W side of the sounds where W-going tide or eddies meet the almost constant swell, or there are strong W'ly winds, the seas are extremely dangerous to small vessels. Chart 2769 should be consulted with care particularly if proceeding out W through the sounds or round the S end of Berneray.

Berneray

General   Berneray has a distinctive wedge shape with a lighthouse on the W side near its highest point. There are rugged cliffs on its S end. Barra Head is the most S'ly part of Berneray. Approaching Berneray in low cloud the loom of Barra Head Light may not be visible even at 0.5M.

Anchorage   Can be obtained in 8m sand, sheltered from the S through W to N winds, out of the tidal streams, just off the storehouse on the N side of Berneray about 2.5 cables SE of Shelter Rock. This anchorage is untenable when a heavy sea is running. Landing may be had at the slip opposite the shed.

Sound of Berneray

General   It is less than 1M across the Sound of Berneray from Mingulay to Berneray. The Sound narrows to less than 3 cables at its W end which can be affected by swell meeting tidal flow, resulting in very heavy seas. **Shelter Rock** (dr 2.4m) lies 0.75 cable off the N end about the middle of the N shoreline of Berneray.

Tides   In the Sound of Berneray and S of the island the streams run as follows:
E-going stream begins —0600 Ullapool (+0205 Dover) and runs for 4.5 hrs. 2.5 knots springs
W-going stream begins —0145 Ullapool (—0605 Dover) and runs for 8.25 hrs. 2.5 knots springs

Passage   In settled conditions a smooth passage can be expected through the Sound, but W, S, or SE of Berneray the effects of tidal flow and swell may result in rougher sea conditions and a distance off of at least 0.5M is suggested. Keeping mid-channel in the Sound easily clears all dangers but beware of heavy seas at W entrance when swell and adverse tidal flow meet. Also at the E end of the Sound turbulence may be experienced when the E-going tidal stream is present with an E wind.

Mingulay Bay   *Charles Tait*

Mingulay

General   This is perhaps the most spectacular of the southern islands with its six small compact peaks and, on the W side, high steep cliffs filled with birdlife.

Caution   Making a landing on Mingulay Bay in a yacht's tender in the ever present swell could cause overturning. When ashore tie dinghies well above HW mark.

Anchorage   It is about 3.5M from Bagh Ban, Pabbay across the Sound of Mingulay to the temporary anchorage at Mingulay Bay. From Castlebay, Barra to Mingulay Bay is about 11 miles. Although landing may be made at either end of the sandy beach, a swell is almost always present even in settled conditions. When landing on Mingulay Bay is difficult in the swell, Skipisdale, about 1M SW around the shore on the Sound of Berneray, may offer a better landing or taking off place.

Interest   Old village on E side of island above Mingulay Bay.

Sound of Mingulay

Tides   In the Sound of Mingulay the streams run as follows:
E-going stream begins +0505 Ullapool (+0045 Dover). 3 knots springs.
W-going stream begins —0140 Ullapool —0600 Dover). 2–2.5 knots springs.

Passage   During passage round Mingulay in settled conditions, a considerable swell may be experienced which is accentuated by tidal conditions on the W side of the Sound of Berneray. Note the Twin Rocks a little over 1 cable W of the most W'ly point on Mingulay and their fountains of white water in the breaking swell.
Give the Twin Rocks a wide berth and, once past Sunk Rock 5 cables further N, there are no dangers if a distance off of 1 cable is kept until the Sound of Mingulay is reached. During the E-going stream a heavy race extends 3.5 cables E from the N point of Mingulay. Pass S of the Outer and Inneir Heisker. There are overfalls on the E side of Mingulay where the E-going tide from the Sounds of Mingulay and Berneray meet.

Caution   In heavy weather the seas break right across from Outer Heisker to Inner Heisker. In such conditions pass S of these islets when making passage through the Sound of Mingulay and avoid the race which extends 3.5 cables E of the N end of Mingulay which is present during the E-going stream.

Pabbay

General

It is about 4M from the anchorage W of Meanish on Sandray across the Sound of Pabbay to Bagh Ban at the SE end of Pabbay but this bay is only suitable for temporary anchorage. Its eastern arm, Rosinish, has many submerged rocks for at least 1 cable off its S end. Give the S end of Rosinish a wide berth on entering Bagh Ban and hold to the W side of the bay. If circumnavigating Pabbay in settled conditions passage can be made between Inner Heisker and the SW end of Pabbay but note Sloch Glansich (dr 3.2m) 1 cable W of the middle of the W side of Pabbay. Once through the channel between Inner Heisker and Pabbay, keeping about 2 cables off clears all dangers including a drying rock 1 cable off the most N'ly point on Pabbay.

Sound of Pabbay

Tides

In mid-channel in the Sound of Pabbay :
E-going stream begins +0505 Ullapool (+0045 Dover). 3.5-4 kn. springs.
W-going stream begins—0140 Ullapool (—0600 Dover).
The E-going stream is strongest during its first 3 hours. The W-going stream is weaker than the E-going. Eddies form both N of Pabbay and S of Sandray in the Sound and these streams begin close inshore 3 hours earlier than in mid-channel.

Passage

If making a passage through the Sound of Pabbay from the W note that there is a rocky bank with a least depth of 8.3m about 6 cables W of Lingay. This bank extends N across the N half of the W entrance to the Sound. The seas on parts of this bank may break dangerously in heavy swell. Greanamul lies about 6 cables further E of Lingay. Beware the rock with 1.3m over it 1.5 cables to the NW of Greanamul.

Approach

Sound of Pabbay from the West
Pass 2 cables N of the most N'ly point on Pabbay and pass S of Lingay and Greanamul. In appropriate sea conditions it should be possible to pass N of Lingay and Greanamul at a distance of at least 2 cables to avoid shallows, particularly off Greanamul. Take care to avoid also a shallow patch about 2 cables S of Sandray.

Sandray & Flodday

General

It is about 5 miles from Castlebay to the bay W of Meanish at the SE end of Sandray. In settled conditions this bay offers anchorage near its head and is a good base from which to explore. Exposed to E'ly winds.

Although the shores of Sandray are worth exploring the following points should be borne in mind. Sgeir Leehinish, an above water rock at the SW end of the temporary anchorage, may be passed on either hand as can Cletta, 3 cables W. Reefs extend well out from the W side of Sandray including extensive reefs round Sheader Rocks and rocks and shoal patches off Rubha Sheader. In the Sound of Sandray, Loimbo Breaker (dr 1.1m) 3.5 cables NW of Sandray must be avoided as should Kerr Patch, 3 cables off NE Sandray shore.

Meanish Bay, SE Sandray   *Charles Tait*

Sound of Sandray

Tides

Tidal Streams in the Sound of Sandray :
E-going stream begins +0505 Ullapool (+0045 Dover). 3 kn springs.
W-going stream begins —0140 Ullapool (—0600 Dover). 2–2.5 kn springs.

Approach

If making a passage through the Sound of Sandray from the W note the W entrance is narrowed by a shoal bank extending 3 cables N of Flodday, over which seas often break, and another extending 3 cables off the SW shore of Vatersay. These shoals make the safe channel a little over 2 cables wide. Loimbo Breaker (dr 1.1m) 3.5 cables NW of Sandray must be avoided and left to starboard.

Before the W end of Flodday bears more than 160°, set a course to bring the N side of Sgeir a Chlogaid in line with the S end of Muldoanich bearing 086°. Sgeir a Chlogaid is 3m high and is the S'most of a chain of above water rocks extending 4 cables S of the SE side of Vatersay. When about 0.5 mile W of Sgeir a Chlogaid, steer to pass either close S of this rock or about 2 cables N of Sandray to avoid Kerr Patch.

Caution

During SE gales an extensive 16m bank directly S of Muldoanich and E of Sandray causes dangerous seas to break.

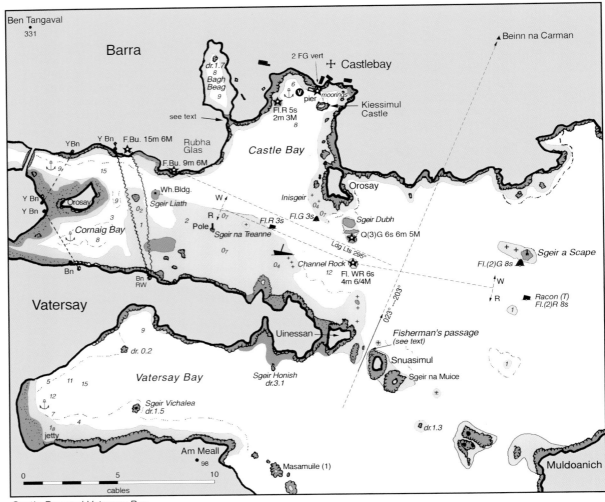

Castle Bay and Vatersay Bay

Castle Bay, Barra

Charts	(ii) 1796 Barra Head to Point of Ardnamurchan	
	(iii) 2769 Barra Head to Greian Head OS31	

General   Castlebay, which can only be reached from the E due to the causeway between Barra and Vatersay, provides a well protected anchorage from winds from all directions. It is the centre of a lively community and is a good base from which to explore the islands to the south.

Visitors moorings, Castle Bay   *Charles Tait*

Offshore Lights	Barra Head Lt Ho	Fl 15s 208m 18M (on Berneray)
	Bo Vich Chuan	Q(6) + LFl 15s S Cardinal buoy
	Curachan	Q(3) 10s E Cardinal buoy
	Within Sound of Vatersay entering from E:	
	Sgeir a'Scape	Fl.(2)G. 8s Green con. buoy
	2 c SE of Sgeir	Fl.(2) R 8s Red can buoy
	a'Scape	Racon (T)

Inshore Lights & marks	Channel Rock	Fl WR 6s 4m 6/4M	Wh. column with R bands
	Sgeir Dubh	Q(3)G 6s 6m 5M	Wh. column with G bands
	Leading lights	FBu. 9/15m 6M	Orange triangles on Wh. lattice twrs on Rubha Glas bearing 295°
	Inisgeir	Fl.G 3s	Green Con. Buoy
	3c W of Inisgeir buoy	Fl.R.3s	Red Can buoy
	Ferry Terminal	2FG.(vert) 3M	
	Lt. 5c WSW of pier	Fl.R 5s 2m 3M	
	Sgeir Liath	Daymark (unlit)	Wh. building
	Sgeir na Treanne	Daymark (unlit)	Pole

Tide   Const. —0108 Ullapool (—0528 Dover)   MHWS 4.3   MHWN 3.0   ML 2.4   MLWN 1.6   MLWS 0.5
Approaching Castlebay from the E the tidal flow does not exceed half a knot in either direction.

Castle Bay, Barra (continued)

Approach From the E pass between Bo Vich Chuan buoy and Muldoanich. Head to pass N of the Red Can Lt buoy, Racon (T) Fl (2) R 8s, but S of Sgeir a'Scape and its ruined beacon showing at half tide marked by a green buoy FL(2)G 8s. Pass between Sgeir Dubh and the white column with red bands marking the Channel Rock awash 2 cables S.

By night the transit orange triangles and lights on Rubha Glas bearing 295° lead safely to the entrance of Castle Bay. There are no leading lights into Castle Bay itself but turn to steer 350° when passing the Inisgeir Fl.G buoy and head for the Lt. Fl.R 5s WSW of the Ferry Terminal. 2 FG vert are shown at the pier.

By day, to avoid Inisgeir, a reef 0.3m above HW and a 1.8 submerged rock N of it and various shallow patches to the SW and W of Orosay, maintain course 295° on the Rubha Glas transit orange triangles until Castlebay pier is open W of Kiessimul Castle by at least the width of the castle rock before turning into Castle Bay. Head to the W of the pier, keeping approximately to the middle of the bay.

Anchorage **Castlebay**. 12 **Visitors moorings** (15 tonnes max) are available. About 1 cable W of the pier near the remains of the old pier in 6m gives good holding clear of the moorings. There is shelter in all winds except strong SE or S winds. The small bay NE of the castle is filled with moorings and small boats and provides poor holding. Note underwater pipes and cables near the N of the castle. Keep clear of the pier as the ferry requires room to manoeuvre and holding is reported poor. In strong SW winds some shelter can be had behind the reef (dr 2.9m) on the W side of the bay clear of moorings. If the anchorage becomes uncomfortable in S'ly winds there is better shelter in **Cornaig Bay** (see p.16) or **Vatersay Bay** (see below). Whilst yachts may tie up at the pier to take on water they must not remain there overnight as the pier is used by fishing boats and the Caledonian MacBrayne ferry.

Bagh Beag on the W side of Castle Bay offers perfect shelter in depths of 2 to 10m. However the entrance has a rocky sill drying 1.5m and on its W side a rock dries 2.9m. Bagh Beag is best entered at slack HW keeping to the E side and leaving the rock at the entrance to port. At other times the strength of the flow may make entry hazardous. Note the drying rock near the head.

Facilities Shops, PO, tel., hotels. Petrol & diesel at garage. Calor gas (tel. 01871 810408), bank, craft shops and laundrette. Water at pier. Car ferry service to Oban and Lochboisdale, S. Uist. Daily air service to Glasgow. PO bus to airstrip near Northbay. Car and bicycle hire. Tourist Information Centre. Golf course.

Interests Climbing and fishing. Visit St Columba's Well. Public library in school. Kiessimul Castle, home of the Clan MacNeil open to visitors. Kilbarr Church and chapel's mediaeval remains near Eoligarry. Dun Bharpa, chambered cairn.

Vatersay Bay

General This bay has the finest sandy beach on the E side of the Outer Hebrides. In addition to the natural beauty of Vatersay Island the bay itself provides excellent shelter except in Easterly winds.

Approach From Castle Bay pass S of Dubh Sgeir and close N of the Red Can Lt buoy Fl (2) R 8s before turning SE to pass round the E side of Muldoanich. Keeping 2 or 3 cables off the S side clears all dangers. Then head for the centre of the bay to clear Sgeir Vichalea (dr 1.5m) off the S shore formerly marked by a beacon which has now collapsed and is not visible at HW. From Castlebay round the E side of Muldoanich to the anchorage in Vatersay Bay is about 7 miles.

There is an alternative **Fisherman's passage** without going E of Muldoanich. This deep water passage lies close W of Snuasimul. The apparently broad passage E of Sgeir na Muice is encumbered with several dangerous rocks.It should be noted that the islet Uinessan is separated from Vatersay only at HW.

When approaching the passage from Castlebay pass S of of Sgeir Dubh with the Rubha Glas leading beacons in line astern on course 115°. Do not turn S until the beacon on Sgeir Dubh and the ruins on the SW side of Orosay bear 335°. Steer 155° until the deep water channel W of Snuasimul opens out.

With Beinn nan Carnan (150m) under the E shoulder of Heaval astern bearing approximately 023°, steer about 203°. The width of the channel at its N end is little more than 50m, being restricted by a drying rock on the NW side of Snuasimul (charted as being above HW but this is not the case). Keep about 20m W of the rocky shore of Snuasimul to clear the rock just mentioned and the submerged rock in the centre of the channel and maintain a course of 203° or thereby.

If proceeding N through the passage from Vatersay Bay to Castlebay note the channel width as described above and maintain a course of 023° towards Beinn nan Carnan until the leading line on Rubha Glas bears 295° in order to avoid the extensive rocks N of Uinessan. From Castlebay to the anchorage in Vatersay Bay is less than 4 miles using the Fisherman's passage.

Anchorage In 5m sand, N of the jetty clear of moorings at the head of the bay W of Sgeir Vichalea on which the former beacon, reported fallen, is not visible at HW. Note the head of the bay shelves steeply especially at the N end.

Facilities Water at standpipe near the red roofed house 150m from the SW corner of the bay.

Sound of Vatersay

General

A causeway connecting Vatersay Bay to Barra prevents a passage through the Sound of Vatersay .

Approach

From the NW the leading line to clear the rocks at the entrance to the Sound is 132° which is the transit of two houses on Vatersay with a road running between them. The SW shore of Barra should not be approached closer than 1c to avoid Bogha na Lighte (dr 0.5m). Leave the leading line before reaching Bo Leahan (dr 1.4m). Anchor in 7 to 11m short of the causeway.

Sound of Vatersay

From the E maintain course 295° from Sgeir Dubh until about 2 or 3 cables from the front orange triangle of Leading Lights on Rubha Glas and the channel N of Sgeir Liath with its white building has opened up. Proceed to the causeway where anchorage may be had off either shore W of the underwater cable.

Cornaig Bay. Pass N of Sgeir Liath with its day mark white building and do not turn S until the second (most W'ly) beacon of the leading lights on Rubha Glas, which has a cable beacon beside it, is abeam. Make for the pipeline beacon on the S shore (about 3 cables S of Orosay) to clear rocks off the NE corner of Orosay as well as the shoal water W of Sgeir Liath. Anchor in 4 to 8m **clear of the pipeline** which crosses the bay marked by beacons at either end. Do not anchor much further into the bay than indicated by the the W side of Orosay as the bay shallows.

Facilities: Water and Diesel at causeway slipway (key card needed, see p. 5).

North Bay, Barra

Charts

(ii)   1796   Barra Head to Point of Ardnamurchan
(iii) 2769   Barra Head to Greian Head
(iii) 2770   Sound of Barra.   OS map 31

General

The SE side of Barra has many drying rocks and shoal patches. This coastline is dangerous and should not be approached except with great care. Maintaining a course of 0.5M to the E of a line joining Bo Vich Chuan buoy and Binch Rock Buoy at the E entrance to the Sound of Barra clears all dangers. North Bay is a well sheltered anchorage on the NE side of Barra, particularly in the inner Bagh Hirivagh. North Bay is about 10M from Castle Bay.

Lights

Bo Vich Chuan	Q (6) + LFl 15s	S Cardinal Pillar buoy
Curachan (Red rocks)	Q (3) 10s	E Cardinal Lt buoy
Binch Rock	Q (6) + Lt Fl 15s	S Cardinal Pillar buoy
Ardveenish (sectored Lt.)	Oc.WRG 3s 6m 9-6M	
Factory pier	2FG vert.8m 4M	

Tide

Const. —0057 Ullapool (—0517 Dover)   MHWS 4.3   MHWN 3.1   ML 2.4   MLWN 1.7   MLWS 0.6

Approach

From the South. From the Bo Vich Chuan buoy to **Curachan**, a distinctively shaped islet off the S side of the entrance to North Bay, is about 2M. The Red Rocks, marked with an E cardinal buoy, extend at least 0.5M N and NE of Curachan. They are dangerous and must be avoided. Keeping 0.5M E of a line from the Bo Vich Chuan buoy to the Binch Rock buoy clears all dangers. Do not turn into North Bay until well clear of the Red Rocks to the N and NE of Curachan, and the bay is well open between Bruernish, Barra and the island of Fuiay. Mid-channel leads safely into North Bay.

From the North. To avoid confusing the Sound of Hellisay for North Bay, maintain a course from Binch Rock buoy to Bo Vich Chuan buoy until Curachan and the E Cardinal light buoy off the Red Rocks to the N of Curachan on the S side of the entrance to North Bay are identified. Do not approach within 0.5M of Curachan. The Red Rocks, an extensive reef, are dangerous. Alter course when North Bay is well open between the island of Fuiay and Bruernish, and leave Beatson's Shoal (depth 2m) to starboard. Alternatively, having carefully identified the Sound of Hellisay S of the islands of Hellisay and Gighay, pass 2 cables S of Flodday and Fuiay to leave Beatson's Shoal safely to port.

From the East. From 5 or 10 M off the summit of Barra, Heaval (382m) may be seen and used as a guide. Closer in, the radio mast S of Bruernish or Curachan give the approximate position of North Bay. Then proceed as above.

Anchorage

Between Fuiay and Black Island in 10m. Note the drying reefs extending more than 1 cable from Black Island, and Fuiay also S from the N end of the bay. Alternatively anchor **W of Black Island** or in **Bagh Hirivagh** in 3m, 2 cables W of the jetty gives the best protection of all but there is a number of small boat moorings. **Note.** The inner approach to Bagh Hiravagh is buoyed (see plan).

Bruernish Bay. On the W shore of North Bay in 4m mud provides good shelter except from the East. Hold to the NW side of the bay to avoid the rocky patch (0.9m).

8/09

North Bay, Barra (continued)

Facilities   Mobile shop, tel. Ardveenish Seafood factory. Water, diesel (large quantities only) and petrol at factory pier. Air service to mainland at Traigh Mhor, less than 2 miles away. Post bus to Castlebay twice daily. No gas but tel. 01871 810419.

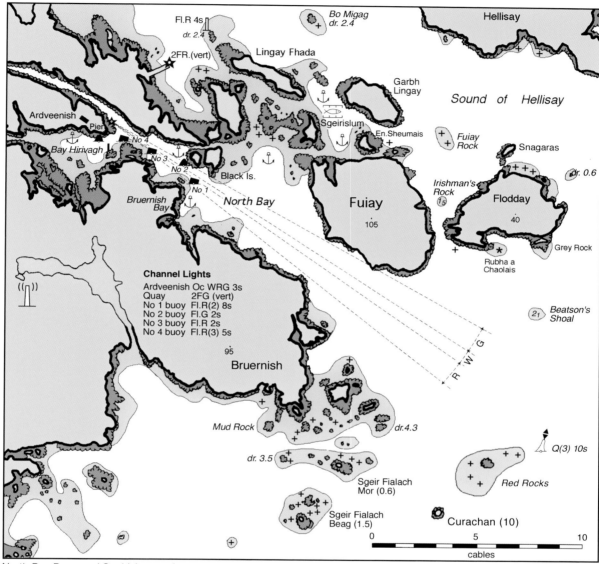

Channel Lights
Ardveenish Oc WRG 3s
Quay   2FG (vert)
No 1 buoy   Fl.R(2) 8s
No 2 buoy   Fl.G 2s
No 3 buoy   Fl.R 2s
No 4 buoy   Fl.R(3) 5s

North Bay Barra and Sgeirislum anchorage

Sgeirislum

General   This small area of water N of Fuiay and W of Garbh Lingay, described in the Admiralty Pilot as an inlet, is bounded by a number of islands and islets which give good shelter from most directions. It is likely to contain a number of fish cages.

Approach   **From the E or NE** through the Sound of Hellisay initially keep mid-channel to avoid a rock (dr 0.6m) 2 cables NE of Flodday then head for the N end of Garbh Lingay, turning S only when the E side of Fuiay is in line with Curachan to avoid a rock 2 cables NE of Fuiay. Pass E and S of Garbh Lingay. The passage between Garbh Lingay and Eilean Sheumais to the anchorage is wide but restricted by reefs extending 100m N from Eilean Sheumais. Hold to the Lingay shore to avoid them.

From the S enter between Fuiay and Flodday keeping to the Fuiay third of the channel to avoid Irishman's Rock (depth 1.5m) mid-way between Fuiay and Flodday. Keeping Curachan open of the E shore of Fuiay will clear the reefs extending NE of Fuiay before heading towards Garbh Lingay and following the passage described above.

There is a W'ward passage between Sgeirislum and North Bay. Rocky shelves extend from both shores. Keep at least 100m off the S Sgeirislum shore. Steer through the passage on a course of approximately 275° but do not alter course until North Bay is wide open to avoid the large area of reefs lying W of Fuiay.

Anchorage   Anchor where shown on plan and clear of fish cages. A tripping line is essential.

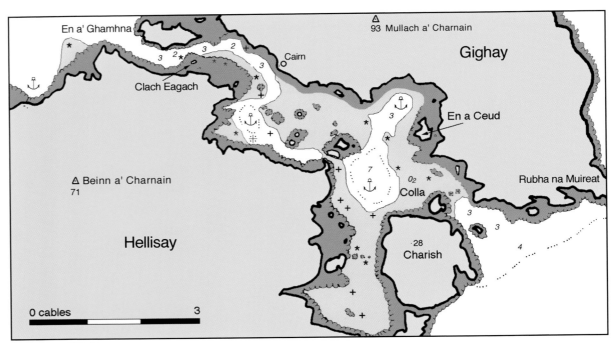

Hellisay and Gighay

Hellisay and Gighay

General
About 9 miles from Castlebay the sound between Hellisay and Gighay provides a challenge for the adventurous yacht skipper. The well sheltered anchorages can be reached from either the E or W side through narrow channels badly restricted by rocks.

Tide
The flood sets into, and the ebb out of, both entrance channels at the same time. The current may reach 2 kn during the first 2 hours of the flood and the ebb.
Const. —0057 Ullapool (—0517 Dover)   MHWS 4.2   MHWN 3.2   ML 2.5   MLWN 1.8   MLWS 0.6

Approach
By the East Sound. This Sound, which is encumbered by a reef stretching across the channel, should only be attempted at least 2 hours after LW and preferably on a rising tide. The entrance to the E Sound is best approached from the SE towards the dip between the high ground of Hellisay and Gighay. When SE of and less than 0.5M off the entrance, the position of the Sound is indicated by the N'ly end of a long finger of low rocks from the Hellisay shore seen against the greenish high ground of Gighay. In the approach to the narrows pass to the E side of the islet E of Charish and then maintain a course slightly E of mid-channel to pass over the rocks and reef E of Colla and then follow round the N Colla shore. Note that there are reefs and rocks extending from the Gighay shore just N of Colla. A sandbank with at least a depth of 0.2m at LWS extends W and SW about 1 cable into the anchorage from N of Colla. The soft sand and shelter offered even at the outer part of the sandbank would seem to present no hazard except to the impatient. **Note** the drying rocks 0.5 cable W and SW of Eileen a Ceud which cover about 1.5 hours before HW.

By the West Sound. From the Sea of the Hebrides keeping 1 or 2 cables N then NW of Gighay clears all dangers. The W entrance is situated at a dip between the high ground on Gighay and Hellisay. Viewed from N of W round to NW the area of the entrance is low lying against the skyline. The entrance is narrow, and seaweed covered rocks extend from both shores particularly where it narrows between Clach Eagach on the S shore and the E side of Eilean a' Ghamhna on the N shore. **The navigable channel is very narrow and should be approached on a rising tide with a lookout at the bow.**

To avoid the reefs extending W from Clach Eagach and especially one which extends NW well into the channel, follow, but not too close in, the Eilean a'Ghamhna shore. The heading when approaching and passing through the narrowest part should be approximately towards Mullach a'Charnain, the W side of the highest point on Gighay. Once through the narrowest part, follow the Gighay shore round keeping well clear of the reefs extending N from Hellisay. Initially heading for the cairn clears rocks from both sides but in order to approach the passage between the reefs to enter the anchorage in the SW corner, the cairn must first be passed on the port beam. Turn to approach the anchorage when a little E of the cairn and the passage in is open between the reefs which are often covered.

Anchorage
Anchor **NW of Eileen a Ceud** under the cliffs of Gighay. This may be squally in N'ly winds. Alternatively anchor anywhere **in the pool NW of Charish** in 7m. If anchoring closer to the shores or manoeuvring in the Sound, the rocks should be fairly easily seen in contrast to the sandy bottom. It is possible, preferably on a rising tide, to pass from the E anchorage to the W anchorage by passing between Hellisay and the S'most islets in the pool. Anchorage with restricted swinging room is possible in the **pool SW of the cairn** near the Hellisay shore.

In the **Outer Oitir Mhor on the NW side of Hellisay** there is a good anchorage in strong winds from S to SE in the bay 2 cables S of the entrance to the West Sound. Anchor in 9m close in to the Hellisay shore in the shelter of Beinn a'Charnain. Leave ample swinging room.

Looking north from Hellisay to Gighay over the anchorage NW of Charish

Jane Routh

The Sound of Barra from Scurrival (Fiaray just left of centre)

Charles Tait

The Sound of Barra

Sound of Barra

Charts
(i)   2722   Skerryvore to St Kilda
(ii) 1796   Barra Head to Point of Ardnamurchan
(iii) 2770   Sound of Barra
OS 31

General
Although this shallow Sound is passable except in very bad weather conditions, great care must be taken to identify the leading marks as it is rock strewn with many shallow patches. The channel through the Sound is narrow in places but has a least depth of 6.7m. Due to the shallow patches and the shifting sands, passage through is best made on a rising tide.

Tide
The incoming tidal streams run in from both the W and E ends of the Sound of Barra simultaneously. The out-going streams behave similarly leaving both ends simultaneously. These streams which are weak and variable meet and separate in Oitir Mhor and W of Eriskay.
The in-going streams begin +0530 Ullapool (+0110 Dover).
The out-going streams begin —0045 Ullapool (—0505 Dover).

The strongest tidal flow in the Sound is experienced in the Drover Channel, N of Fuday. The **NW-going stream** sets towards Drover Rocks. The **SE-going stream** sets towards Fuday with overfalls extending for half a mile E'wards.

Approach
Approach from the East
Weaver's Castle (43m), a ruin on the S end of Stack Islands about 0.75 mile S of Eriskay, makes a conspicuous reference mark for ascertaining position before passing through the Sound from E to W.

Approach from the West
Pollachar Inn, a two-storey house, stands on the shore at the SW end of South Uist. The Inn can be seen from the SW, W and NW directions of approach. The Kate Beacons are situated on the N side of Fiaray (West beacon, white stone, diamond topmark; East beacon, white stone wooden triangle topmark).

Caution
No attempt should be made to navigate E and N of a line from Washington Reef through Outer Hasgeir to Big Rock (dr 0.9m) which lies 3 cables W of Lingay.

Passages
Westward Passage from the Sea of the Hebrides to the Atlantic Ocean
The main channel, which is marked by the Binch Rock buoy (S Cardinal Pillar buoy) in the approach, is between the N end of Gighay and Weaver's Castle at the S end of the Stack Islands. From the SE there is a danger of mistaking the Sound of Hellisay for the main channel. Enter the Sound from S of Binch Rock steering course 327° only when the W side of Orosay (28m) is just open of the E side of Lingay (49m). After passing Bogha Tanna (dr 0.9m), marked by an E cardinal buoy, continue for 4 cables, and before reaching McGillivray Patch turn onto a course of 277° when the sandy patch on Fiaray is in line with the most N'ly point of Fuday. This course clears McVean Rock. Once past McVean Rock alter course to starboard to acquire the leading line of the Kate beacons on Fiaray. Note the SE going tidal set and overfalls mentioned above. Once the Kate Beacons on Fiaray are on a leading line bearing 273°, follow this course westwards through Drover Channel leaving Drover Rocks S card. buoy to starboard. When Dunan Ruadh, the most W'ly point on Fuday bears due S (180°), steer 330° with the summit of Fuday astern. To avoid the Inner Temple Rock do not turn into Temple Channel (course 267°) until Ben Scrien (183m) is in line with the S'most end of Lingay bearing 087° astern.

Temple Channel's leading marks are distinctive and its water comparatively smooth, breaking only when the heaviest seas are subjected to a weather-going tidal stream. The marks leading through the Washington Channel are indefinite and in heavy weather this channel will have breaking seas nearby.

Eastward Passage from the Atlantic Ocean to the Sea of the Hebrides
If approaching the Sound of Barra from the SW or W, the Sound is not easily identified until well open when the sharp peak of Beinn Scrien on Eriskay should bear 085° showing N of Fiaray. **If approaching from the NW keep well clear of Washington Reef.** Though the Sound be well open, do not approach until Benn Scrien, Eriskay, is in line with the S end of Lingay bearing 087°. If planning to use the comparatively smooth water of Temple Channel with its distinctive marks, proceed on course 087° into Temple Channel, N of Fiaray, leaving Temple Rock to port and Inner Temple Rock to starboard until the summit of Fuday bears 150°. Approach Fuday on course 150°. Turn E and follow course 093° only when Kate Beacons on N Fiaray are in line astern 273°. Proceed on this course through Drover Channel leaving Drover Rocks to port. Be aware that the SE-going tidal stream sets towards Fuday and sets up overfalls extending for half a mile E'wards from the NE end of Fuday.

If making for Outer Oitir Mhor, once through Drover Channel and clear NE of Fuday with the high ground of Gighay and Hellisay clearly identified, head for the mid-point of Gighay and Hellisay on a course of about 160°. Cat Rock (dr 0.3m) about 1 mile E of the E side of Fuday will be left to port.

Sound of Barra continued over

Sound of Barra (continued)

Caution

When altering to the course of 160° parallel to the NE coast of Fuday do not overrun to the E'ward towards the Cat Rock (dr 0.3m) but keep 2 cables off the coast of Fuday to avoid the Goose Rocks.

If making for the Sea of the Hebrides, maintain an E'ly course 093° until the E side of Lingay bears due N (000°) then alter course 137°. To avoid McVean Rock on the starboard hand and McGillivray Patch on the port hand, alter to course 097° when the N extremity of Fuday and the sandy patch on Corran Ban, Fiaray, are in line astern 227°. Take care not to overshoot this transit. Maintain the course of 097° until the SW extremity of Orosay is open of the NE extremity of Lingay before turning to course 147° which takes you into the Sea of the Hebrides S of Binch Rock.

Alternatively the E'wards passage can be commenced through the Washington Channel but this channel although deeper, has less distinctive leading marks and there is the risk of badly breaking seas in heavy weather and it is not recommended.

Anchorage

On the W side of the Sound of Barra
The **Sound of Fiaray**, for emergency use only, is situated between the most N'ly point on Barra and the island of Fiaray. The Sound is entered from the W only. On entry, keep in the southern half of the sound as a reef extends fully 1 cable S of the SW end of Fiaray and there are two rocks in the centre. Anchor in at least a depth of 4m when sufficiently out of the swell.

Outer Oitir Mhor

General

Whilst the E end of Outer Oitir Mhor is free of dangers the W and S sides have many rocks including the extensive reefs near Greanamul and Bull's Rock. Though there is safe passage from Outer to Inner Oitir Mhor to the Sound of Hellisay, it should be piloted with care.

The buoys as shown on the plan which mark the route taken by the Ferry between Eriskay and Barra greatly assist navigation in this area.

Keep 2 cables off the N and W sides of Greanamul. If proceeding between the W entrance to the anchorage at Hellisay Gighay keep at least 2 cables N of a line between the entrance and Greanamul to avoid dangerous unmarked rocks E of Greanamul.

Anchorage

Cordale Beag at the S end of Fuday where there is a fresh water stream. Note there is a rock in the middle of the bay.

Sound of Eriskay

Chart

(iii) 2770   Sound of Barra

General

The Sound of Eriskay as a navigable channel to the W has been closed by the causeway between Eriskay and South Uist. The Sound has many reefs, sandbanks and shoal patches and it would be dangerous to approach the causeway from the West without local knowledge.

Approach

From the NE or E guard against Bogha Reme (dr 1.5m) and Rubha Dubh Rock (dr 1.5m) both about 2 cables off the South Uist shore between Rubha Melvick and Rubha Dubh, the NE entrance to the Sound. Note also the submerged rock about 5 cables NW of Hartamul.

Enter the Sound between Calvay and Rubha Dubh. Initially keep 2 cables from the South Uist shore to clear Rubha

Sound of Eriskay

Dubh rock before closing to 1 cable to avoid the cables and the wreck if proceeding towards the NE corner. Do not attempt to go further W than this without Chart 2770.

Prior to the causeway being built, beacons were established for the benefit of the Eriskay Ferry. One on Bank Rock, on the sandbank close to the N side of Eriskay, is on the W side of a passage through the bank, and makes it possible, after half flood, to approach Haun on Eriskay, where there is a 3m pool inside the sandbank.

Facilities

At Haun. (see opposite)

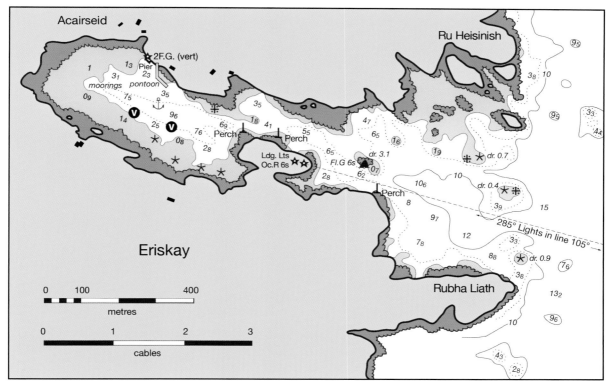

Acairseid Mhor, Eriskay

Eriskay

Chart   (iii) 2770 Sound of Barra

General   9 miles from Lochboisdale, S. Uist, Acairseid Mhor on the E side of Eriskay offers protection from winds from all directions and is an outstanding natural harbour.

Tide   Const. —0052 Ullapool (—0512 Dover) MHWS 4.2 MHWN 3.2 ML 2.5 MLWN 1.8 MLWS 0.6

Lights   Acairseid Mhor. Ldg Lts Oc.R.6s bearing 285° Front and Rear 26m from front. Posts on Wh. painted bases.
G buoy Fl.G.6s positioned S of rock (dr 3.1m). Radar reflectors on perches on the S side of the entrance channel.

Approach   **From the S** keep mid-channel between Stack Islands and Galeac, a 3m high rock. Eilean Leathan, the most S'ly of the islands, has Weaver's Castle (43m), a fairly conspicuous ruin, on its SW end. Maintain this mid-channel course 2 cables off the islands and Eriskay shore to leave Roderick Rock (dr. 0.6m) 2 cables to starboard. Alternatively keeping a little over 1M E off the E side of Eriskay clears all dangers until Acairseid Mhor opens up.

When E of Rubha Liath there is a choice to be made to clear the drying rocks in the approach; **either** to pass 30m N of Rubha Liath, which is steep-to, to clear the drying rock (dr. 0.9m) 60m to the N, **or** to pick out the leading line bearing 285° on the transit beacons indicated on the plan. This latter course passes between two drying rocks but the beacons are not easily seen against the evening sun and the inshore course may be preferred.

Once W of the entrance rocks and heading for the inner anchorage, proceed mid-channel leaving the rock in the centre of the channel (dr. 3.1m), marked by a G buoy Fl.G.6s, well to starboard. There is a rock ridge, with a least depth of 1.5m, N of mid-channel at the entrance to the anchorage (see plan). Two perches on the S shore mark the extremities of rock ledges. Pass 20-30m off the inner perch.

From the N pass 2 cables NW of Hartamul (25m) and head towards Eriskay. Make for a point E of Rubha Liath and proceed as for the approach from the S. **Caution.** If passing E and S of Hartamul keep at least 0.75M off to avoid the Red Rocks (dr. 0.3m) which extend up to 5 cables S of Hartamul.

Anchorage   In the basin clear of moorings wherever sufficient depth may be found. Buoying the anchor is recommended as old moorings lie to the W of the pier. **2 visitors moorings** are available (max 15 tonnes).
Caution. Anchoring and manoeuvring inshore of the visitors' moorings is to be avoided (see plan above)

Facilities   Water is available by hose at the pier where there is a pontoon. Diesel is also available (key card needed, see p.5). Calor gas, tel., PO, pub. Stores from the shop at Haun (1M). Causeway for vehicles links Eriskay with South Uist. Ferry service to Barra across the Sound of Barra.

Interest   The Eriskay Pony is now unique to the island. The very fine Prince's Strand (Coilleag a'Phrionnsa) on the W side of Eriskay is where Prince Charles Edward Stuart (Bonnie Prince Charlie) first landed on Scottish soil in July 1745. The film 'Whisky Galore' was based upon the wreck of 'The Politician' in the Sound of Eriskay.

Rubha Melvick to Loch Skipport

Charts
(ii) 1795 The Little Minch
(iii) 2770 Loch Boisdale
(iii) 2825 Lochs on the East Coast of Uist (includes Loch Eynort, Loch Skipport and Loch Carnan)
(iii) 2904 Usinish to Eigneig Mhor
OS 31 and OS 22

General
South Uist has an E coast which is of rugged appearance with mountains, hills and vertical cliffs to the sea. The W side of South Uist is flat and inhabited. The steep rocky shores of the E side are penetrated by three sea lochs each in its own way providing anchorage. Loch Boisdale offers safe anchorage with facilities. Of the two remote lochs, Loch Eynort is wild and somewhat inaccessible except in favourable weather and tidal conditions, whilst Loch Skipport is easy of access and offers many well protected anchorages.

Lights
Ushenish Lighthouse	Fl WR 20s 54m W 19M/R 15M	Wh Twr
McKenzie Rock	Fl.(3) R 15s	Red can buoy 3M ESE of Loch Boisdale
Loch Carnan landfall	L.Fl.10s	(RW) Pillar buoy

Marks

Hills and mountains of South Uist
The Boisdale Hills from S to N consist of Beinn Ruigh Choinnich (272m), Triuirebheinn (355m), Stulaval (372m), and Arnaval (250m). This group lies between Loch Boisdale and Loch Eynort.
The Benmore Mountains consisting of Bheinn Mhor (618m), Ben Corodale (525m) and Hecla (604m) form a significant group in the N half of South Uist.
South of Loch Boisdale there is a third group of smaller hills between 160m and 250m in height.
Ushenish Lighthouse is located in a position which is slightly more N'ly than the summit of Hecla, the most N'ly of the Benmore group.

Tides
Const, —0052 Ullapool (—0512 Dover)
Range: 3.6m Sp, 1.3m Np
N-going stream begins +0520 Ullapool (+0100 Dover)
S-going stream begins —0040 Ullapool (—0500 Dover)

In the sea area E of Loch Boisdale and S to Rubha Melvick, the SE point of South Uist, there exists in the in-coming tide a complex system of tidal streams. This creates an eddy, present only during the NE-going stream, which moves SW from Rubha na h'Ordaig, the S entrance to Loch Boisdale towards Rubha Melvick. As a consequence of this eddy on the NE-going tide, the stream always runs SW from Rubha na h'Ordaig to Rubha Melvick for up to a mile off. These tidal streams, in strong winds, may result in awkward or even dangerous seas extending up to 5 miles E from Loch Boisdale.

Off Loch Boisdale the tidal streams are the same as between Berneray and the Sound of Barra.
N-going stream begins +0520 Ullapool (+0100 Dover)
S-going stream begins —0040 Ullapool (—0500 Dover)
The spring rate off the headlands at Loch Boisdale and Loch Eynort is from 1.5 knots to 2 knots in each direction but is less in the bays between the headlands. The streams lose strength offshore but in strong wind over tide conditions an offing of at least 2 miles is recommended.

Off Loch Eynort the tidal streams begin 30 minutes later than off Loch Boisdale.

Loch Skipport looking seawards towards Shillay Mor (p. 31)

Jane Routh

Approaches to South Uist

Ushenish Lighthouse   *Charles Tait*

Passage

From N of Canna to the East Coast of South Uist

From Canna the shorter passage is along the N coast of Canna. This avoids rocks off the SW end. From N of Canna the most likely view of the Outer Hebrides is no view (!), but in good visibility, particularly in clear N'ly airstreams, the view can be startlingly clear. Looking on an arc from the NW to W, the Benmore group, the most formidable group, is seen. Then there is the gap at Loch Eynort separating the Boisdale Hills from the Benmore group. Another gap to sea level at the entrance to Loch Boisdale precedes the third set of smaller peaks. From N of Canna these 3 sets of peaks would subtend a horizontal angle of about 20°.

Landfalls

The most S'ly gap leads to Loch Boisdale, the gap between the Boisdale Hills and the Benmore group to Loch Eynort, and N of the Benmore group, lies the entrance to Loch Skipport. Note Eaval (345m) on North Uist's SE coast may be seen during the passage. It is very distinctive.

From the South Keeping 2 miles E of a line from Rubha na h'Ordaig S of the entrance to Loch Boisdale, to the headland at Usinish and the landfall safe water buoy at Loch Carnan, clears all dangers. Between Rubha Melvick and Rubha na h'Ordaig there are rocks extending about 4 cables off-shore.

North of Loch Boisdale, Stuley Island lying 1 mile S of the entrance to Loch Eynort has rocks extending 4 cables off its SE and E shores. The Broad Rocks extend 3 cables N of Stuley. S of Stuley Island lies Sgeir an Fheidh (3m) close inshore with a drying rock 0.5 cable offshore. **At night Ushenish Lt shows red over these hazards.** *Note: Ushenish refers to the light, Usinish is the point itself.*

From the North The Benmore Mountains on South Uist would indicate the general position of Ushenish Lighthouse. Loch Skipport entrance is about 2 miles N of the lighthouse. To enter Loch Carnan, find the safewater buoy (LFl l0s) marking the entrance to Bagh nam Faoileann and locate the lit channel buoys leading in to the loch

Bagh Hartavagh

General

The shore from Rubha na h'Ordaig 1 mile NE to Meall an Isagaich, the E entrance to Bagh Hartavagh, has several drying reefs extending 4 cables offshore. Shoal patches extend 4 cables N from the E entrance half way to McKenzie Rock Lt Buoy, Fl (3) R 15s. Although these shoals have at least depth of 6m they make the entrance to Bagh Hartavagh dangerous in bad weather.

Approach

Best from the N from McKenzie Rock buoy.

Anchorage

The bay is muddy and rock strewn 3 or 4 cables from its head but some shelter may be found up to 2 cables within the entrance. Anchor in 3m. Exposed to the NE.

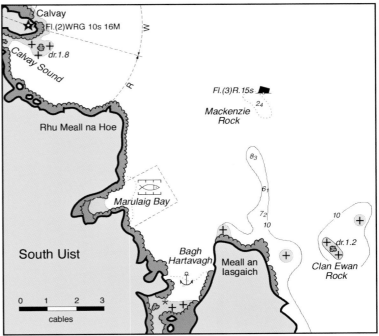

Bagh Hartavagh, Loch Boisdale

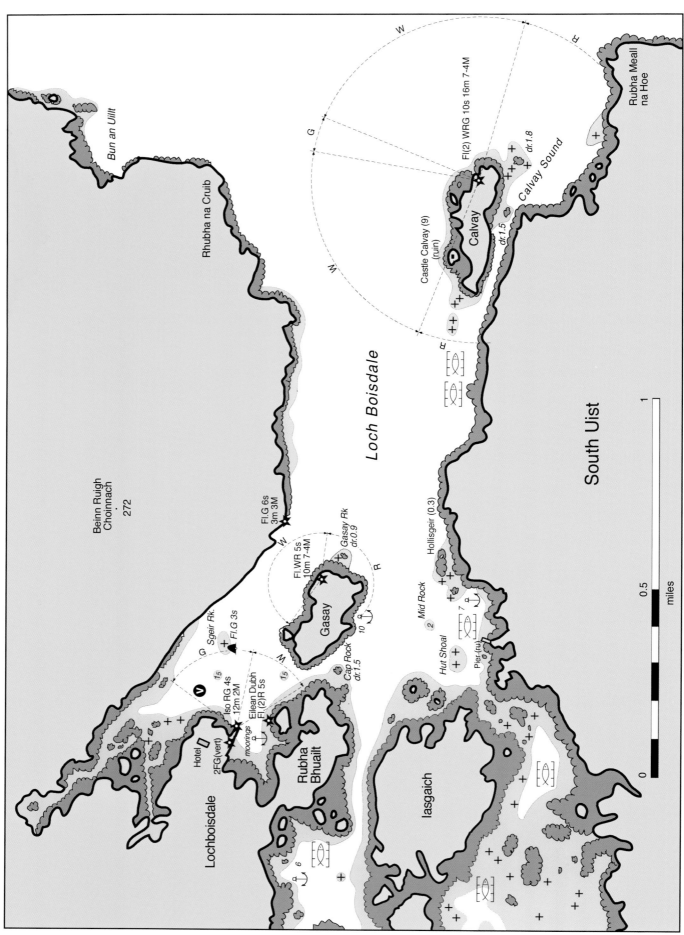

Loch Boisdale and approaches

Loch Boisdale

Charts	(ii) 1795 The Little Minch
	(iii) 2770 Loch Boisdale
	OS 31

General Lochboisdale, one of the main centres of population, is situated on the N side of Loch Boisdale about 21 miles N of Castlebay. The greater part of the loch westward of Lochboisdale consists of countless islands and reefs, most of which dry and little of it is navigable.

Tide Const. —0052 Ullapool (—0512 Dover) MHWS 4.3   MHWN 3.0   ML 2.4   MLWN1.6   MLWS 0.5
The streams in the entrance and in the navigable part of the loch are barely perceptible.

Lights

Outside Loch Boisdale

McKenzie Rock	Fl.(3) R 15s	Red can buoy 3M ESE of Loch Boisdale

At the entrance to Loch Boisdale

Calvay Lt Bn	Fl.(2) WRG 16m 7/4M	Wh framework Twr

Within Loch Boisdale

Gasay Lt Bn	Fl WR 5s 10m 7/4M S	Wh framework Twr
N shore Lt Bn	Fl.G 6s 3m 3M	Metal Post
Sgeir Rock	FL G 3s	G. Con. Lt buoy at N side of channel to Ro-Ro terminal
Bn. 0.25c N of Eilean Dubh	Fl (2) R 5s 2m 3M	
Ro-Ro Terminal	Iso RG 4s 12m 2M	On pier
	2 FG (vert) 8m 3M	On dolphin

Approach It is important not to confuse Loch Eynort with Loch Boisdale, both having low skylines at their entrances. Approaching from the E, the S shore is comparatively flat near sea level at the entrance whilst the N side is much steeper with rugged rocky ravines rising from the entrance shore to the prominent cone shaped Beinn Ruigh Choinnich (272m).

From the N the approach is straightforward **but from the S**, to avoid rocks and shoal patches, it is best to keep at least 1 mile E of Rubha na h'Ordaig until Loch Boisdale opens up N of McKenzie Rock buoy. Turn W to pass N of this buoy, Calvay and Gasay. If tacking beware of rocks extending 2 cables W of Calvay and one cable E of Gasay further in.

At night shoal banks, offshore rocks and McKenzie Rock are covered by the red sector of Ushenish Lt between bearings 356° and 013° and by the red sector of Calvay Lt bearing more than 286°. Approach both Calvay and Gasay in the white sectors but do not get too close. Head for the Ro-Ro Ferry Terminal with the green channel buoys to starboard.

Anchorage **Bagh Dubh** SW of the Ferry Terminal. Whilst it is important to anchor clear of the ferry pier (At night fishing boats use it and the ferry is normally berthed here overnight) do not go too close to Eilean Dubh on the SE corner as a reef extends from it. Many local moorings. Poor holding ground is reported in the middle of the bay. In SE gales swell can reach the pier in which event anchor W of Rubha Bhuailt. (see below)

6 visitors moorings (max 15 tonnes) are available in the arm of the loch E of the terminal. Beware of the rocks N of the moorings

SW of Gasay. Close in. Not recommended in strong W or SW winds. If approaching from the pier note Cap Rock (dr 1.5m) in mid-channel between Rubha Bhuailt and Gasay. Keep to the Gasay side.

W of Rubha Bhuailt. From the pier pass close W of Gasay to avoid Cap Rock and then head to pass between Rubha Bhuailt and Iasgaich. Do not alter course N into the bay until clear of extensive reefs off the SW corner of Rubha Bhuailt. At LW note the submerged rock NW of Iasgaich. This is a quieter anchorage than Bagh Dubh but it is much encumbered with fish farms

S side of Loch. In the bay E of the ruined pier. Approach with the E side of Gasay in line with the peak of Beinn Ruigh Choinnich to avoid various rocky hazards. Anchor in 4m to the W of the fish farm.

Facilities **At Lochboisdale:** Hotel, shops, PO, tel. Tourist information Centre with shower facilities, Bank. Water at pier. Car hire. Car ferry to Oban. Bus to Benbecula Airport. Golf course.
At Daliburgh: 3 miles W : Supermarket, PO, tel, calor gas.

Interest **At Lochboisdale:** Prince Charles' cave on hillside above Bun an Uillt at N side of entrance. In settled conditions anchor in bay. Ruins of mediaeval castle on Calvay at mouth of the loch.
At Daliburgh: Ruins of underground houses (wheel-house AD 300-400) on the machair.

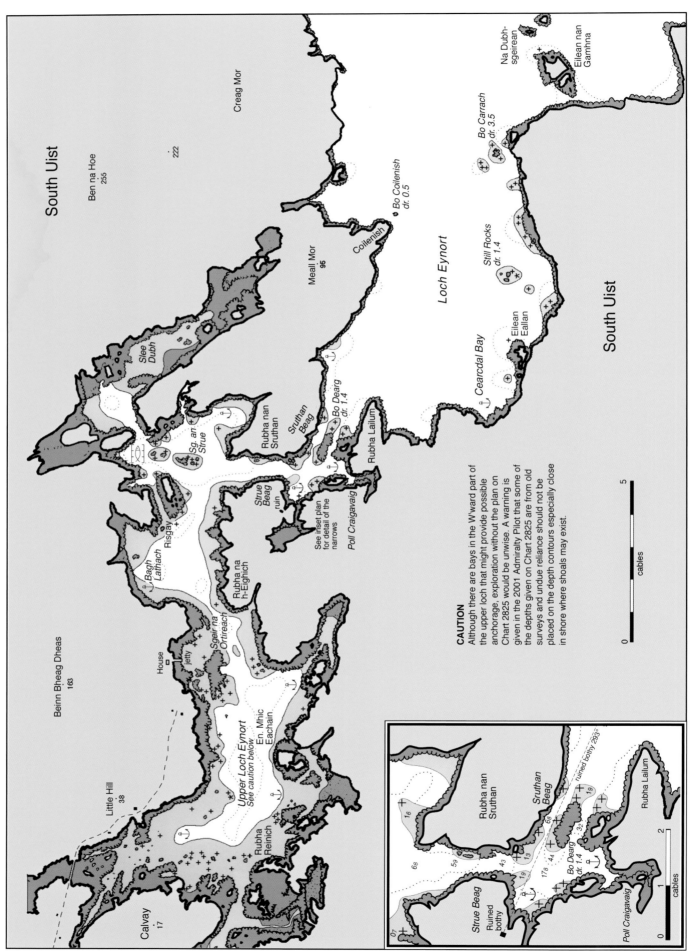

South Uist

Ben na Hoe
255

Creag Mor

·222

Beinn Bheag Dheas
163

Slee
Dubh

House

jetty

Little Hill
38

Calvay
·17

Bagh
Lathach

Risgay

Sgeir na
Ortireach

Upper Loch Eynort
See caution below

Rubha na
h-Eighich

Rubha
Reinich

En. Mhic
Eachain

Sg. an
Srue

Strue
Beag

ruin

Rubha nan
Sruthan

Sruthan
Beag

Bo Dearg
dr. 1.4

Meall Mor
95

Coilenish

Bo Coilenish
dr. 0.5

Poll Craigavaig

See inset plan
for detail of
the narrows

Rubha Lailum

Loch Eynort

Cearcdal Bay

Still Rocks
dr. 1.4

Eilean
Eallan

Bo Carrach
dr. 3.5

Na Dubh-
sgeirean

Eilean nan
Gamhna

South Uist

CAUTION
Although there are bays in the W'ward part of
the upper loch that might provide possible
anchorage, exploration without the plan on
Chart 2825 would be unwise. A warning is
given in the 2001 Admiralty Pilot that some of
the depths given on Chart 2825 are from old
surveys and undue reliance should not be
placed on the depth contours especially close
in shore where shoals may exist.

0   cables   5

Rubha nan
Sruthan

Strue Beag
Ruined
bothy

Sruthan
Beag

ruined bothy 293°

Bo Dearg
dr. 1.4

Rubha Lailum

Poll Craigavaig

16
68
59
43
13
1.9
4.4
0.7
6.8
17.8
1.9
3.2

0   cables   2
1

Loch Eynort

Charts   (ii) 1795   The Little Minch
(iii) 2825   Lochs on the East Coast of Uist.   OS map 22

General   Upper Loch Eynort offers views of barren slopes in wild isolation. Westwards, low horizons can be seen contrasted with the steep lines of Sheaval and Trinival rising from the shores. The upper loch is difficult and at times even dangerous to enter. The outer loch is not protected from E'ly winds. If awaiting the tide for entry to Loch Eynort there are anchorages in the Outer Loch in Caercdal Bay and in a bay on the N shore. It is about 8 miles from Lochboisdale to the narrows in Loch Eynort.

Caution   On the E side of the Benmore Mountains the slopes descend steeply almost to the shore. Even in moderate W'ly winds strong gusts are experienced. In strong winds these gusts are most violent.

Tide   Const. —0035 Ullapool (—0455 Dover) MHWS 4.3   MHWN 3.0   ML 2.4   MLWN 1.6   MLWS 0.5
At the entrance to Loch Eynort
In-going stream begins +0545 Ullapool (+0125 Dover).
Out-going stream begins —0035 Ullapool (—0455 Dover).

Nowhere in the outer part of Loch Eynort do streams gain any perceptible strength except at Sruthan Beag, the narrow channel leading to Upper Loch Eynort. (for details see below)

Approach   Although Loch Eynort, like Loch Boisdale, has a low skyline in the vicinity of its entrance the latter's shores are steep to particularly on the N side. Loch Eynort's skyline is low at the entrance to the upper loch.
From the S give Glas-eilean Mor and Dubh-sgeir Mhor, both islets 2 cables E of Stuley, a fair berth to avoid a drying rock off their N shores. Once clear of Cleit a'Ghlinn-mhoir and Na Dubh-sgeirean, both islets on the S side of the entrance, head for Meall Mor whose slopes end in distinctive vertically indented cliffs and mark the entrance to the upper loch. If tacking, beware of Bogha Coilenish (dr 0.5m) 0.5 cable off the N shore and Bogha Carrach (dr 3.5m) and the Still Rocks (dr 1.4m) 0.5 and 1 cable respectively off the S shore. Once clear of these hazards, head for the anchorages or if tide and conditions are suitable make the passage into the upper loch.
From the N head to pass midway between Bogha Coilenish (dr 0.5m), 0.5 cable off the N shore and Bogha Carrach (dr 3.5m) 0.5 cable off the S shore. Once clear of Still Rocks (dr 1.4m) on the S shore, head for the anchorages with due regard to the tide and weather conditions.

Anchorage   **Caercdal Bay** in the SW corner of the outer loch about 1 cable W of Eilean Eallan off the burn. If closer to the island beware of the submerged rocks off its W end. Exposed to the E.

In the **bay 2 cables E of the N entrance to Sruthan Beag** in 4m out of the tide. Good holding but exposed to the SE.

Upper Loch Eynort

General   The entrance channel, **Sruthan Beag**, is difficult and could be dangerous unless care is taken to ensure that tidal conditions are favourable. The 1894 Admiralty Pilot gives LW as the best time for entering the upper loch and just before HW for leaving to return to the outer loch.

Tide   In-going stream begins —0615 Ullapool (+0200 Dover)
Out-going stream begins —0010 Ullapool (—0430 Dover)
The spring rate in both directions is reported to be between 5 and 7 knots. There are overfalls in the channel and eddies at either end. During the out-going stream the flow runs strongly across Bo Dearg until it uncovers. In the upper loch tidal flows are weak.

Approach   As will be seen from the plan the Sruthan Beag channel is extremely narrow and encumbered with rocks the largest being Bo Dearg (dr. about 1.4m), a large flat seaweed-covered rock. To pass through the narrows on the N side of Bo Dearg follow the N shore 20m off, from a point opposite two distinctive white patches on the rock face of the N shore, until clear of Bo Dearg then as the inner leg of the channel leading N begins to open head W to clear a 1.3m patch extending about 0.25 cable W at the SE entrance. Once open, head N into the narrows maintaining a mid-channel course until the Upper Loch is reached.

Alternatively instead of making for the Upper Loch turn S when well clear of Bo Dearg to enter **Poll Craigavaig** where, out of the main tidal flow, the inner half of Sruthan Beag may be observed before completing the passage.

Caution: On the outward passage beware of a drying rock at the SE end of the inner channel and keep clear of the nearby 1.3m patch extending about 0.25 cable. Guard against being swept towards Bo Dearg.

Anchorage   **Poll Craigavaig** in the SE area W of the first narrows provides anchorage in moderate depths. There is a fish farm here. **Alternatively** the NW corner off the ruined cottage provides anchorage in 2m.

In **Upper Loch Eynort the first bay E of the inner narrows** has a rock at the centre of its entrance. Pass N and E of this rock. Well sheltered anchorage in 4 to 7m in shingle. Do not be tempted to proceed N when leaving the narrows as this is an area strewn with rocks. Moving westwards from the narrows to **Bagh Lathach**, which provides anchorage in 3 to 5m, avoid the reefs and rocks extending up to 1 cable SW off Risgay. **See the Caution** on the plan opposite for anchorage and exploration of the W'ward part of the Upper Loch.

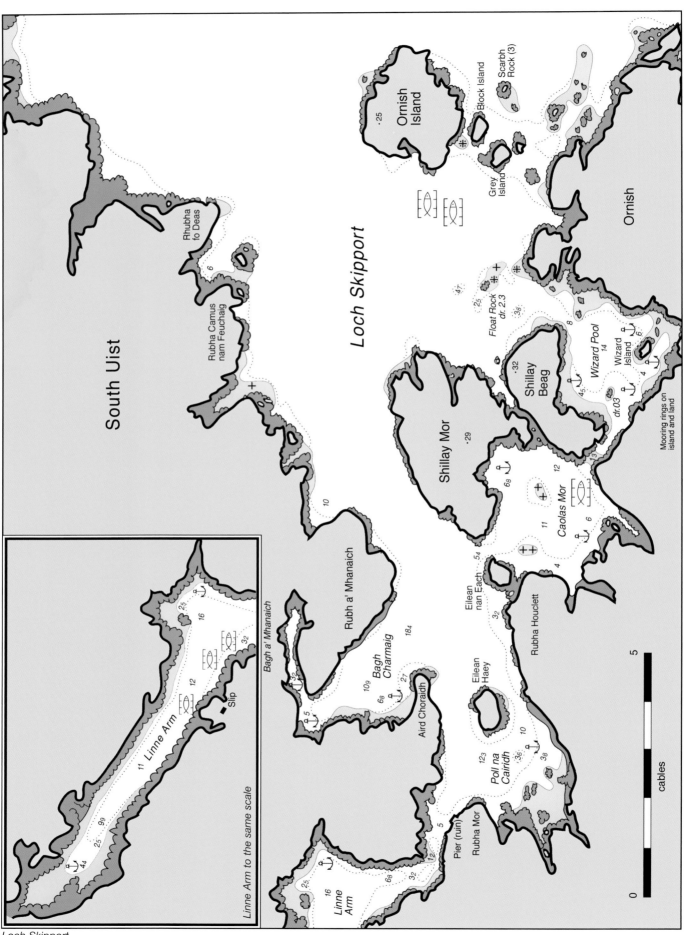

South Uist

Loch Skipport

Rhubha fo Deas

Rubha Camus nam Feuchaig

6

10

Ornish Island

·25

Block Island

Scarbh Rock (3)

Grey Island

⚓

Ornish

Float Rock dr. 2.3

⚓

·47

·25

·3.8

8

Wizard Pool 14

Wizard Island

6

dr.0.3

·45

·32

4

Mooring rings on island and land

·3

Shillay Mor

Shillay Beag

·29

6.8

12

Caolas Mor

6

11

·54

Rubh a' Mhanaich

Eilean nan Each

·32

·32

Rubha Houclett

Bagh Charmaig

18.4

10.9

27

6.8

·3.2

Aird Choraidh

Eilean Haey

12.3

·36

10

·38

Poll na Cairidh

5

Pier (ruin)

Rubha Mor

12

6.8

·3.2

Linne Arm

16

·25

Inset:

Bagh a' Mhanaich

·25

16

·32

Linne Arm

12

11

Slip

·25

9.9

4.4

Linne Arm to the same scale

0

cables

5

Loch Skipport

Loch Skipport

Charts
(ii) 1795 The Little Minch
(iii) 2825 Lochs on the East Coast of Uist
(iii) 2904 Usinish to Eigneig Mhor
OS22

General
Loch Skipport is situated to the N of the Benmore Mountains at Hecla's N slopes. It is easy of access offering in its friendly almost rock free shores, well protected anchorages. Hecla, the austere, dark mountain, can send down some awesome gusts in SW or SE fresh to strong winds. Loch Skipport entrance is about 14 miles from Lochboisdale.

Loch Skipport, McCormack Bay anchorage   *Jane Routh*

Tides
Const. —0052 Ullapool (—0512 Dover) MHWS 4.6 MHWN 3.3 ML 2.5 MLWN 1.7 MLWS 0.5
In the entrance to Loch Skipport the streams run as follows:
In-going stream begins +0545 Ullapool (+0125 Dover)
Out-going stream begins —0035 Ullapool (—0455 Dover)
Inside the loch the flow rates are imperceptible or weak even in the narrow channels.

Lights
There are no lights or marks inside or outside Loch Skipport apart from Ushenish Lt Ho Fl WR 20s 54m 19/15M about 2 miles S of the entrance.

Approach

From the S
Keeping 1 mile off shore clears all dangers. In fresh to strong winds keep well offshore below the Benmore Mountains and 1 or 2 miles off the headland at Usinish in wind against tide conditions. The entrance to Loch Skipport is about 2 miles N of Ushenish Lighthouse. To enter do not use the false entrance S of Ornish island but pass to the N.

Once within the loch the approaches to the anchorages are free of danger except for Float Rock (dr 2.3m) at the N entrance to Wizard Pool. In general the shores can be closely approached.

From NE or E
As the land to the N and W of Loch Skipport is low-lying, locate the Benmore Mountains and Ushenish Lighthouse and proceed as from the S.

Anchorage
Wizard Pool Approaching from N the Float Rock (dr 2.3m), a large flat reef, lies at least 1 cable E of both Shillay Mor and Shillay Beag and presents no danger if the shores of Shillay Mor and Shillay Beag are followed. Entering the pool, note the reefs extending almost a cable from the Ornish shore hence keep to the Shillay Beag shore but not too close as reefs extend from its SE end. Anchor anywhere within the pool in suitable depth but beware of a rock (dr 0.3m) more than 0.5 cable E of the SE shore of Shillay Beag.

If anticipating fresh to strong SW or SE winds with their violent gusts descending the slopes, more shelter could be had by anchoring as close as possible to the S shore W of Wizard Isle. In addition a line ashore might add to peace of mind. A slop is experienced in this anchorage when the wind is N or NE.

It is possible, except at LW springs when the least depth is 1.3m, to pass from Wizard Pool into Caolas Mor (Little Kettle Pool) S of Shillay Beag.

Caolas Mor (Little Kettle Pool) Approaching from W of Shillay Mor the entrance is straightforward. Note the two groups of submerged rocks shown on plan. Anchor in suitable depth. Wizard Pool is less subject to gusts in fresh to strong winds from the S'ly quarter. For passage between the two pools see above.

Poll na Cairidh This bay lies SE of the ruined pier The drying rocks inshore are avoided by anchoring in not less than 5m. May be subject to weed.

Linne Arm When entering the narrows W of the pier of Rubha Mor keep closer to the S shore to avoid a 1.3m patch off the N shore. Anchor anywhere in suitable depth but note rocks dry about 0.5 cable offshore in some parts of the arm.

Bagh Charmaig (McCormack Bay) has no dangers even close inshore except 2 reefs, one off the SW entrance, Aird Choraidh, and the other halfway along the W side. Anchor at head of bay in 5m or in 3m just within **Bagh a'Mhanaich** (Mannoch Arm) which shoals further in. Holding is poor (soft mud) and this N'ly area of Loch Skipport is subjected to severe squalls in S'ly weather.

Facilities
None. Water at burn in SE corner of Caolas Mor.

Loch Skipport to Loch Carnan

Charts
(ii) 1795   The Little Minch
(iii) 2904   Usinish to Eigneig Mhor
(iii) 2825   Lochs on the East Coast of Uist, Plan of Loch Carnan
OS 22

General
From Luirsay Glas to Loch Carnan, a distance of about 3 miles, a large number of islets, reefs, rocks and channels extend from the NE coast of South Uist shore as much as a mile into Bagh nam Faoileann. Chart 2904 is essential when approaching the anchorages on this short length of coast.

Tides
Const. —0040 Ullapool (—0500 Dover) MHWS 4.5   MHWN 3.2   ML 2.6   MLWN 1.9   MLWS 0.6
The tidal streams are weak and nowhere exceed 1.5 knots.

Mark
Loch Carnan Power Station, a long low, twin chimney building visible from N of Luirsay Dubh

Anchorage
Caolas Luirsay At N side of entrance to Loch Skipport a narrow channel between Luirsay Dubh and the South Uist shore. Neither the S or NE entrances would be easy in waves of any significant size as they are narrow with a depth of only 2.1m in the NE channel and less in the S. Note submerged rock 0.3m towards N end of pool. Not recommended except in settled weather. Anchor in 7m mud.

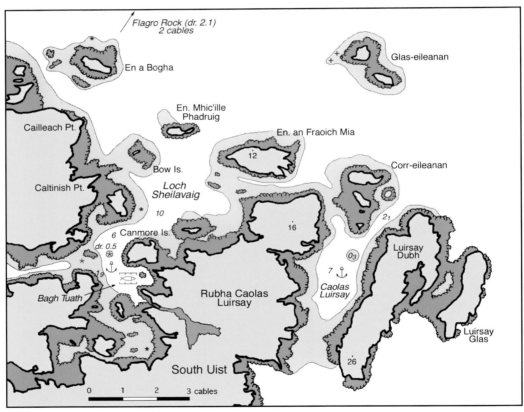

Caolas Luirsay and Loch Sheilavaig

Loch Sheilavaig

Approach
From the S there is a passage S of Glas Eileanan, a double island set on a reef NE of the entrance. Pass N of Luirsay Islands, Corr-Eileanan and Eilean an Fraoich Mia and turn to port when the latter island and Eilean Mhic'ille Phadruig open. If in doubt, a bearing astern of 062° on the W side of Glas-eileanan leads to the entrance (course 242°). Now identify, 4 cables within the entrance, Canmore Island, named on Chart 2904 as En a' Chinnbhaoraigh, which looks like a peninsula. Pass N and then W of Canmore Island. A rock (dr 0.5m) lies about 100m W of Canmore Island; do not go too near the island's rocky shore when avoiding it. The bottom is clear and kelp on rocks can be seen.

Anchorage
Bagh Tuath, S of Canmore Island in 4m mud. Beware of the reef in the E half of this bay.

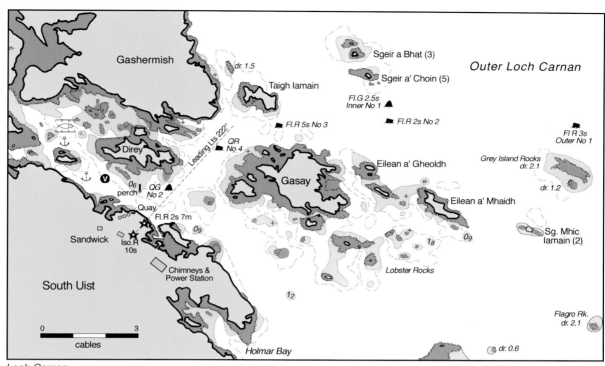

Loch Carnan

Loch Carnan

Charts   (iii) 2904   Usinish to Eigneig Mhor
               (iii) 2825   (Plan of) Loch Carnan

General   Loch Carnan, about 5 miles from Loch Skipport, is the N'most anchorage on South Uist before South Ford, an impenetrable barrier for all but the smallest craft. Loch Carnan has many islets, reefs and channels on its E side. There is a light-buoyed channel N of Gasay. The two chimneys of the power station and the oil tanks near the quay on the S shore are conspic.

Tide   Const. —0040 Ullapool (—0500 Dover) MHWS 4.5   MHWN 3.2   ML 2.6   MLWN 1.9   MLWS 0.7
              Tidal streams do not exceed 1.5 kn.

Lights   **Outer approach buoys**
              Bagh nam Faoileann   L.Fl.10s   Pillar buoy (RW) in position 57° 22.30'N, 7° 11.46'W
              Outer No 1   Fl.R. 3s   Red can light buoy 1 cable N of Grey Island Rock
              Approach Channel buoys - see plan
              Leading lights bearing 222°   Front: Fl.R 2s 7m 5M   These are on posts with Wh diamonds and R stripes
                                            Rear: Iso.R 10s 11m 5M

Approach **From the S** keep on a N'ly course until 1M past the Luirsay Islands leaving Glas Eileanan to port. Having identified the Safe Water landfall buoy (RW) L.Fl 10s alter towards the Outer No.1 R buoy Fl.R 3s positioned N of the extensive Grey Island Rocks most of which dry 2.1m. These rocks and buoy must be left to port and the Channel buoys as shown on the plan should then be identifiable. Set course between the buoys and acquire the leading line 222° on the two posts, with white diamonds and R stripe, close SE of the quay. (For lights see above.) The conspic. two chimneys of the power station are 400m E of the quay and are visible from N of the Luirsay Islands. The approach channel passing S of Gasay cannot be recommended without the plan on Chart 2825.

              From the N pass E of Bo Greanamul using the clearance bearing of 193° on Luirsay Glas (S of the entrance to Loch Carnan) well clear of Wiay. Keep 3 cables off Wiay until the chimneys of the power station at Loch Carnan bear 245° when course can be altered to pick up the two inner buoys close SE of Sgeir a' Choin (5) which mark the entrance channel. Then follow directions as above.

Anchorage **One visitors mooring.** Anchor 2 cables **NW of the quay** avoiding shoal water and reef extending 1 cable S from Direy, the S extremity of which is marked with a perch, or alternatively in 8m in suitable depth clear of moorings. Also **W of Direy** but short of the fish farm symbol shown on the plan. The inner section of the loch is studded with reefs. Anchorage space usually available in 4-5m **E of the quay** but note the 0.9m patch shown on the plan NE of the power station.

Facilities None except for water at quays. Supermarket 4M. Restaurant 1M

Peter's Port to Flodday Sound

Charts
(ii) 1795   The Little Minch
(iii) 2904   Usinish to Eigneig Mhor
OS 22

General
The coastline between South Uist and North Uist is occupied mainly by the Island of Benbecula. This is a much indented shore with many islands such as Wiay, Ronay, Floddaymore, Floddaybeg and Lochs such as Loch a'Laip, Loch Keiravagh, Loch Uiskevagh and innumerable islets, reefs, rocks and narrow channels extending E from Benbecula.

Passage
Between Hecla (604m), South Uist and Eaval (345m) on North Uist the coast outline is low lying and lacks dominant features. Keeping a mile off shore from Luirsay Glas, Loch Skipport, along this coast easily clears all hazards. The coast should not be approached in poor visibility or in E'ly winds which are fresh to strong as many of the entrances are difficult or even dangerous. In such conditions it is far better to head for Loch Skipport, South Uist or Loch Maddy, North Uist and explore this fascinating coast in settled conditions and in good visibility. The distance from Loch Skipport to Loch Maddy is about 18 miles.

Tides
Offshore the tidal streams run as follows:-
N-going stream begins +0520 Ullapool (+0100 Dover)
S-going stream begins —0040 Ullapool (—0500 Dover)

Inshore the tidal streams run as follows:-
Between South Uist and Benbecula at South Ford:
In-going stream begins +0535 Ullapool (+0115 Dover).
Out-going stream begins—0025 Ullapool (—0445 Dover)

Loch Uiskevagh:
In-going stream begins +0550 Ullapool (+0130 Dover)
Out-going stream begins —0020 Ullapool (—0440 Dover)

Between Benbecula and North Uist at North Ford:
In-going stream begins +0535 Ullapool (+0115 Dover)
Out-going stream begins —0025 Ullapool (—0445 Dover)

Marks
All the following require good visibility for correct identification:

Dominant features which can be seen from afar (from S to N): Hecla (604m) at NE end of South Uist; Eaval (345m) at SE end of South Uist.

Features of some distinction not obviously seen (from S to N): Usinish Point on NE end of South Uist; Ben Tarbert (166m) near head of Loch Skipport; The summit of Wiay, Beinn a'Tuath (100m) a smooth gently rounded outline; Rueval (123m), Benbecula, low outline and Stiaraval (52m) very low outline; Beinn Rodagrich (97m), S end of Ronay; Beinn an t-Sagairt (113m); Ronaybeg (72m), N end of Ronay.

Islets to help identify entrances (from S to N)
Greanamul Deas (10m) for Loch a'Laip, Loch Keiravagh and Loch Meanervagh. This islet has a green rounded shape. Greanamul (16m) for identification of Loch Uiskevagh, Caolas Wiay Beag immediately to the W, and the approaches to Kallin from the S.

Dangers
Dangers less than a mile off shore for entrances (from S to N)
An Dubh-sgeir a Deas (1m) and Du'Sgeir a'Tuath (1m) both at SE coast of Wiay
Bo Greanamul with associated tidal rip 4 cables SE of Greanamul Deas (10m)
Morrison's Rock lies 0.5 mile S of Ronay and 4 cables ENE of Maragay Mor
Ritchie Rock lies 4 cables E of SE Ronay and 7.5 cables ENE of Rubha na Rodagrich, Ronay
The reefs and rocks 1.5 cables off Eileen an Fheidh and close to the E side of Ronay

Admiralty Pilot Bearings to clear the above dangers (from S to N)
Bo Greanamul—Luirsay Glas bearing 193° and well open E of Wiay leads E of Bo Greanamul
Morrison's Rock—The summit of Wiay bearing 200° and open E of Greanamul leads E of Morrison's Rock. Approaching anchorages at Kallin – Steer for Rubha na Rodagrich, Ronay on a bearing of not more than 313° until clear of Morrison's Rock. Rueval, Benbecula bearing 268° and open N of Maragay Beag also leads N of this rock.
Ritchie Rock—Rueval (123m) Benbecula bearing 263° and open S of Rubha na Rodagrich leads S, and Madadh Mor, North Uist bearing 013° and open E of Floddaymore, leads E of both Ritchie Rock and Morrison Rock.
Eilean an Fheidh reefs and rocks, Ronay—The E extremity of Floddaymore bearing 013° leads E of these dangers.

Caution
The channel between Ritchie Rock and Ronay should not be used.

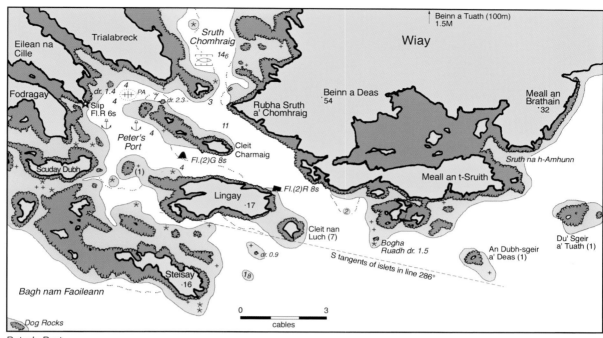

Peter's Port

Peter's Port

Chart   (iii) 2904 Usinish to Eigneig Mhor

General   Peter's Port, an anchorage lies between Benbecula and Wiay and is a little over 4 miles from Loch Skipport and about 3 miles from Loch Carnan. It presents wide skyscapes over South Uist and to the west.

Tides   Const. —0040 Ullapool (—0500 Dover) MHWS 4.6   MHWN 3.3   ML 2.5   MLWN 1.7   MLWS 0.5

Approach   **From the S** make for Beinn a'Tuath (100m), the summit of Wiay. When crossing entrance to Bagh nam Faoileann, alter course for Beinn a Deas (54m) on SW Wiay. The entrance is between Bogha Ruadh (dr 1.5m) and an islet to the W, Cleit nan Luch (7m). A shallow patch extends 0.5 cable S of Bogha Ruadh. Enter closer to Cleit nan Luch leaving it to port.

From the N keeping 0.5 mile off SE coast of Wiay clears both Du Sgeir a'Tuath (1m) and An Dubh-sgeir a Deas (1m) and their off-lying rocks. Heading for S end of Steisay till the entrance opens, clears Bogha Ruadh (dr. 1.5m) and the shallow patch 0.5 cable S of it. Enter between Bogha Ruadh and Cleit nan Luch, an islet 3 cables to the W keeping closer to the islet.

The channel into the anchorage is buoyed S of Cleit Charmaig. Passing N of Cleit Charmaig is to be avoided due to the drying rocks and the tidal stream, also the presence of a wreck (PA) lying SE of the rock (dr. 1.4m) (see plan). The wreck may uncover at LWOS.

Anchorage Anchor SE of the ruined pier, now used as a slip, taking care to avoid the wreck. This slip has 2.4m alongside.

Facilities At Hacklet 5 miles along the road from the pier. Shop, telephone and bus.

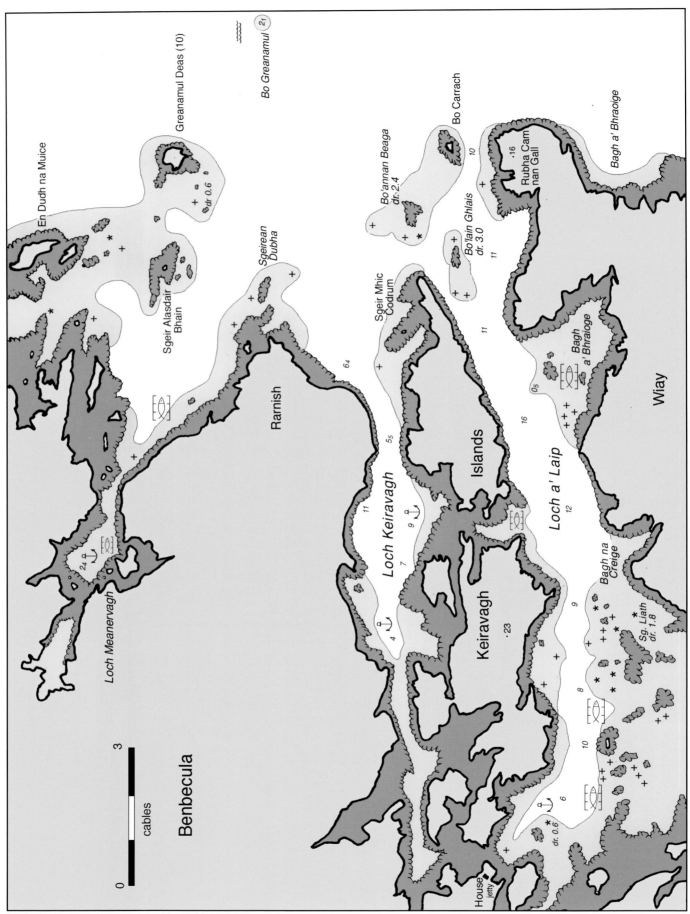

Loch a'Laip, Loch Keiravagh and Loch Meanervagh

Loch a'Laip and Loch Keiravagh

Chart (iii) 2904 Usinish to Eigneig Mhor

General The Keiravagh Islands lie close N of Wiay. Anchorage in adjacent lochs can be found both S and N of the Keiravagh Islands, in Loch a'Laip and Loch Keiravagh respectively. The entrances have many rocks and islets to negotiate. Greanamul Deas (10m) a rounded green islet, is N of the entrances and helps to identify them.

Tides Const. —0040 Ullapool (—0500 Dover) MHWS 4.6   MHWN 3.3   ML 2.5   MLWN 1.7   MLWS 0.5

Approach **From the S** Keeping more than 0.5 mile off the S of Wiay clears both An Dubh-sgeir an Deas (1m) and Du'Sgeir a'Tuath (1 m) and off lying rocks. Once clear of these, the E side of Wiay can be approached to a cable off until Rubha Cam nan Gall, its NE extremity, is reached. Note the position of Greanamul Deas (10m) and, 4 cables E, Bo Greanamul, a dangerous submerged rock with 2.1m over it and associated tide rips.

From the N Pass E of Ritchie Rock which is about 0.5 mile E of Ronay. Identify but do not yet approach Greanamul Deas (10m) in line with Beinn a'Tuath (100m), the summit of Wiay bearing 208°. Note the dangerous submerged rock, Bo Greanamul with 2.1 in over it and associated tide rips 4 cables E of Greanamul Deas (10m).

Luirsay Glas, the N entrance to Loch Skipport, well open of Wiay bearing 193° clears E of Bo Greanamul. Open up either loch for the final approach. **Alternatively** keep 2 cables E of Maaey Glas and approach the loch entrances close E of Greanamul Deas clear of Bo Greanamul.

To enter Loch a'Laip
Best entered before half tide when Bo'annan Beaga and Bogha Iain Ghlais will show. Pass S of Bo Carrach and keep mid-channel. Tend to the N shore only when entering the inner loch N of Sgeir Liath with its extensive outcrops of rocks. **Note:** On leaving Loch a'Laip it helps to identify Greanamul Deas (10m), the rounded green islet, correctly before proceeding N along this rocky and much indented coast.

Anchorage **Near head of loch** in 3m mud in NW arm avoiding rock (dr 0.6m). S of this rock in deeper water allows more swinging room, with S point of entrance just closed behind Keiravagh Island. Excellent shelter but some tidal stream.

Bagh a'Bhraoige has limited swinging room in 3m because of a fish farm and rocks. **Bagh na Creige** is also suitable.

To enter Loch Keiravagh
From the S pass well clear E then NE of Bo Carrach to avoid Bo'annan Beaga (dr 2.4m) and the shallow patch of rock (1.5m) extending NW for 1 cable. Coming **from the N** keep closer to Greanamul Deas (10m) to avoid Bo Greanamul but avoid rocks extending a cable S of Greanamul Deas. The outer entrance to Loch Keiravagh, a cable wide, is between submerged rocks extending 1 cable N from Bo'annan Beaga and 1 cable S from Sgeirean Dubha. When 1 or 2 cables S of Greanamul Deas steering a course of about 235° towards Sgeir Mhic Codrum, an above water rock in the reef strewn N bay of the E'most island, will lead safely between the submerged rocks. When N of Sgeir Mhic Codrum tend to the Rarnish shore to avoid the reef and rock extending NW more than 1 cable from Sgeir Mhic Codrum.

Anchorage Once through the first narrows, anchor in 10m at the opening between the islands. Better protection may be had anchoring in 4m just E of the second narrows.

Loch Meanervagh

Approach Assume a position 2 cables S of Greanamul Deas, 2 cables E of Sgeirean Dubha. With Sgeirean Dubha and the Rarnish shore to port and the rock (dr 0.6m) off Greanamul Deas and Sgeir Alasdair Bhain to starboard, good judgement is needed to set a course to clear these dangers when hidden. When closer to the entrance and clear of the rocks and reefs, follow the Rarnish shore. The entrance to the inner part of the loch is narrow but in settled conditions is not difficult for small manoeuvrable yachts.

Anchorage A fish farm dominates this small anchorage but, once within, it offers good shelter from all directions.

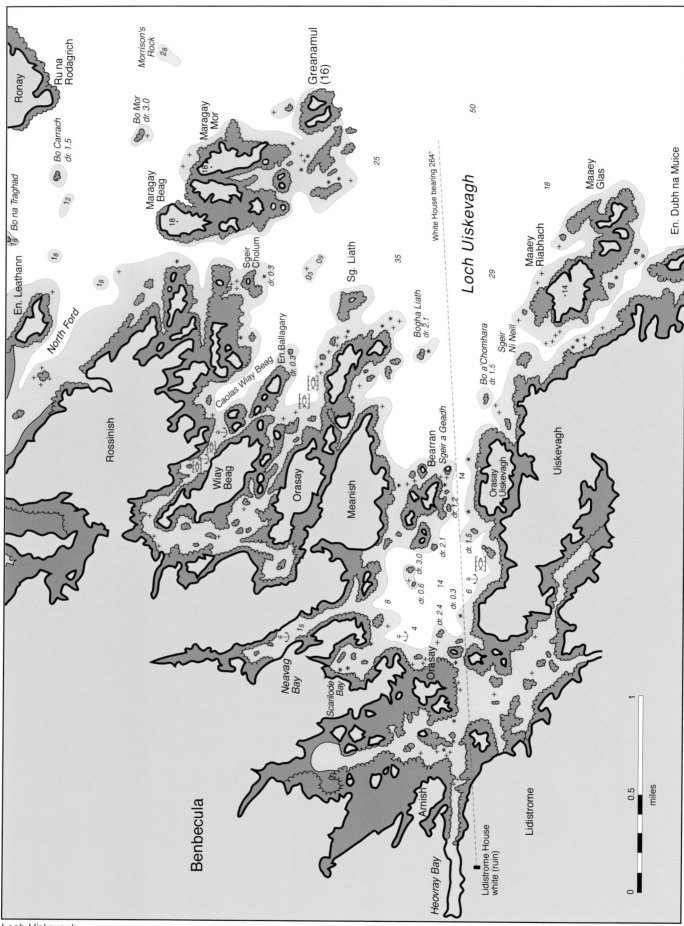

Loch Uiskevagh

Loch Uiskevagh

Chart (iii) 2904 Usinish to Eigneig Mhor

General Loch Uiskevagh is the innermost extent of the sea's penetration of the E side of Benbecula with innumerable islets, reefs and rocks and narrow channels. Great care must be exercised to reach its well sheltered but isolated anchorages. At HW Loch Uiskevagh appears as a broad open firth encumbered with green islets and which, at LW, becomes an almost continuous ridge of bare rocks.

The low-lying nature of the shoreline may make it difficult to identify its features. Viewed from a mile E of Bearran, the eye is subtly led to the entrance to the inner loch at the lowest point on the skyline, by the gently sloping and receding shorelines from Meanish to the W and Uiskevagh in the S. A more obvious pointer is the combined S slopes of Rueval (123m) and Stiaraval (52m) which indicate the entrance to the inner loch. Entry is made between Bearran and Orosay Uiskevagh, a passage 0.5 cable wide. Once within, careful pilotage is needed to avoid the many reefs and drying rocks extending from all shores, particularly W almost to the centre of the loch from Bearran.

Loch Uiskevagh is about 3 miles N from Loch a'Laip and 3 miles S from Kallin.

Tides Const. —0040 Ullapool (—0500 Dover) MHWS 4.8   MLWN 3.6   ML 2.8   MLWN 1.9   MLWS 0.7
The streams are weak everywhere in the loch.

Approach **From the S** keep E of a line through Rubha Cam nan Gall, the NE point of Wiay, Greanamul Deas and Maaey Glas, the most E'ly of Maaey group of islets. This clears all hazards off this shore except Bo Greanamul, a dangerous submerged rock with associated tide rips. (see pp. 34, 36) The outer loch is entered between the Maaey group of islets in the S and Greanamul (16m) group to the N.

Heading NW to identify the entrance or looking for the white house at the head of the loch which provides a leading line of 264° note a large reef with Bogha Liath (dr 2.1 m) at its N end 0.5 mile E of Bearran. Approach to pass S of Sgeir a'Geadh at SE extremity of Bearran. (See below 'Entering Inner Loch')

From the N Keep at least 0.5 mile off the Ronay shore to avoid Ritchie Rock and its associated tide rips and giving Greanamul (16m) a good berth, head SW to identify the entrance or pick up the bearing 264° on the White House at the head of the loch. Note a large reef with Bogha Liath (dr 2.1 in) at its N end 0.5 mile E of Bearran. Approach to pass S of Sgeir a'Geadh at SE extremity of Bearran.

Entering Inner Loch
Pass S of Sgeir na Geadh maintaining a course 264° until W side of Orasay Uiskevagh is just open. Then alter course to 290°, in general direction of S slopes of Rueval, to avoid a drying rock (dr 1.5m) and a submerged rock 2 cables NW of Orasay Uiskevagh. Do not alter course too soon as reefs and a rock (dr 1.2m) extend 1 cable S and W of Bearran into the channel. Keep the heading of 290° towards Scarilode Bay until W of the centre of the loch. With such a low lying shoreline the various islets, headlands and bay entrances are difficult to identify.

Anchorage **Neavag Bay** may be approached when its W side bears 350° or so; alternatively with Scarilode Bay well open on the port beam but clear of the submerged rock SW of the entrance (depth 0.3m). Approach Neavag Bay with caution as reefs extend into the ever narrowing entrance. Well protected but open to the winds. Note the rocks at the head of the bay.

Scarilode Bay has a jetty, suggesting that it was once regularly used, but it is full of reefs and no directions can be given.

Anchorage may also be had in the bay 3 cables **W of Orasay Uiskevagh** in 6m or nearby keeping clear of reefs and drying rocks. Anchoring close in shore with kedge anchor to prevent swinging might offer some protection from SW winds.

Caolas Wiay Beag

Chart (iii) 2904 Usinish to Eigneig Mhor

General Wiay Beag, an island 1 mile NE of Loch Uiskevagh close S of Rossinish, the NE extension of Benbecula, provides good shelter in isolation on the NE side of the island.

Tides Range: 3.9m Sp, 1.3m Np. Const. —0040 Ullapool (—0500 Dover)

Approach From S and N it is best to approached from well S of the Greanamul group of islets with their W extending reefs. A large area of submerged rocks is situated 0.5 mile from the outer anchorage. They lie between a large reef, Sgeirean Liath, a small part of which always shows, and the large reefs W of Greanamul. Passing 1 cable E of Sgeirean Liath on a NW course (315°) clears dangers including a rock (dr 0.3m) a cable SE of Eilean Ballagary at the S side of the entrance. Maintain this course heading for the Rossinish shore until entrance opens out. Once within the outer anchorage N of Eilean Ballagary head to pass E then N of the 2 islets protecting the inner anchorage. Keep mid-channel as reefs extend particularly from the N shore.

Anchorage In the inner anchorage behind islets in 2m. Further in behind Wiay Beag in 4m may offer better shelter but fish farms restrict swinging room.

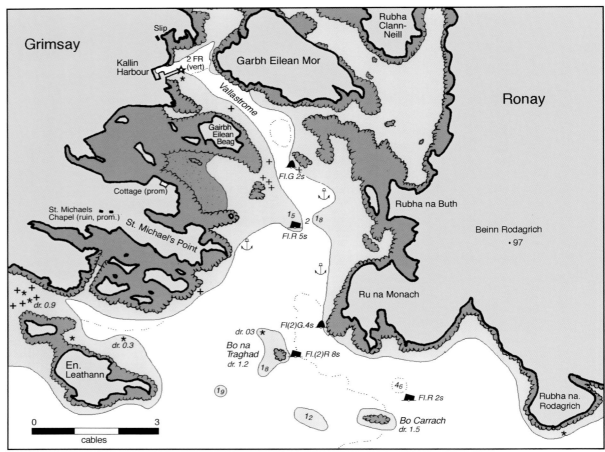

Kallin

Kallin

Chart   (iii) 2904 Usinish to Eigneig Mhor

General   A small fishing boat harbour on Grimsay on the N side of the North Ford, which separates Benbecula from the islands of Grimsay and Ronay to the N. The North Ford extends S and W of the channel leading to Kallin and cannot be navigated safely W of Eilean Leathann. A causeway blocks the North Ford from the W.

Tide   Const. —0040 Ullapool (—0500 Dover) MHWS 4.8   MHWN 3.6   ML 2.8   MLWN 1.9   MLWS 0.7
In-going stream begins +0535 Ullapoool (+0115 Dover)
Out-going stream begins —0025 Ullapool (—0445 Dover)

Lights   Kallin Harbour   2FR.(vert) 6m 5M   Metal column
Light buoys as shown on plan.

Approach   **From NE** keep at least half a mile off to pass E of Ritchie Rock (depth 0.6m) and its attendant tide rips (see pp. 34, 36) then approach as from E. (see below)

     From S pass half a mile E of of Morrison's Rock (depth 2.8m) with Rubha na Rodagrich, the S extremity of Ronay, on a bearing not more than 313° and then continue approach as from E.

     From E aim to pass no more than 1 cable S of Rubh na Rodagrich to avoid Morrison's Rock and Bogha Mor (dr. 3.0m) which lie 3 cables NE of the Maragay group of islets. Identify the R buoy (Fl.R 2s) marking Bogha Carrach (dr 1.5m) then follow the channel marked by port and starboard buoys. The minimum depth in the approach is 2.0m, at the inner port hand buoy (No.2). When entering the Vallastrome keep mid-channel between Garbh Eilean Mor and Garbh Eilean Beag to avoid the reef and shoal water NW of Garbh Eilean. Just before reaching the harbour keep clear of Garbh Eilean Mor to avoid a shoal patch.

Anchorage   **Kallin Harbour** is small and usually well filled with local boats but the recently completed pier allows more room for visiting yachts provided they are prepared to raft alongside fishing vessels. Depth alongside the pier is 4.0m. Anchoring off the pier can cause obstruction and is not recommended as the tidal stream is troublesome.
NW of Ru na Monach. The bay N of Ru na Monach is shoal and anchoring in the channel is almost inevitable.
St Michael's Point. On the W shore in 4m is preferable. Shoal draft yachts may find good shelter in the pool NW of the Fl.R 5s port hand buoy. To enter the pool hold close to the islet N of St Michael's Pt.

Facilities   Water at pier. Diesel (key card needed, see p.5). Travelling shop on Thursdays. Sea food available from factory at pier.

Flodday Sound

Chart   (iii) 2904 Usinish to Eigneig Mhor

General   This narrow inlet between Ronay and
Floddaymore provides many possible
anchorages which can be reached
only by way of the Sound of Flodday.
The entrance N of Floddaybeg is rock
strewn and only used by small local
fishing boats. Eaval (345m), a
mountain on the SE end of North Uist,
indicates the general direction of
Ronay and Floddaymore Islands.

Tide   Const. —0040 Ullapool (—0500
Dover) MHWS 4.8 MHWN 3.6 ML
2.8 MLWN 1.9   MLWS 0.7
The tidal flow in the sound is not
strong but off the entrance a sea is set
up even in moderate winds. This
makes the entrance uncomfortable
during the out-going stream and even
dangerous in strong winds.

Approach   From the S keep at least 0.5 mile off the
Ronay shore to avoid Ritchie Rock and
its associated tidal rip. As reefs and
rocks extend 2 cables E from Eilean an
Fheidh at the S side of the entrance, do
not alter course for the entrance to the
Sound until it is well open. Proceeding
N into Flodday Sound keep to the
Floddaymore side until abeam Rubh an
Traibh. Beyond this point keep to the
Haunaray side of mid-channel but not
too close as reefs extend from there
also. Note particularly the rock 0.5
cable NE of Haunaray.

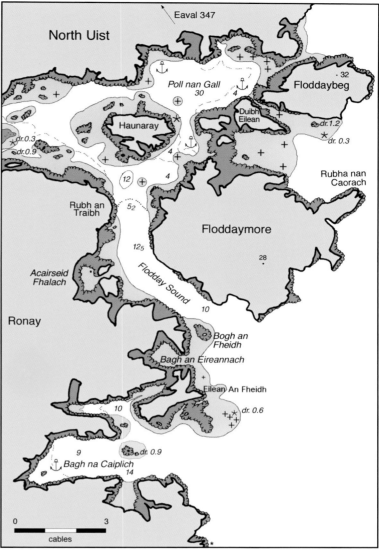

Flodday Sound

Anchorage In the bay **SE of Haunaray**, W of Duibh-eilean. If using **Poll nan Gall** on the N Uist shore note the rock at the W
entrance to the bay. The passage between the rock at the W entrance to Poll nan Gall and the most N'ly reef
extending from Haunaray is 0.5 cable wide but the area beyond the passage is rock strewn.

Acairseid Fhalach on the W side of Flodday Sound, can be entered with caution between the two islets at the
entrance where there is a reported depth of 3.5m by an earlier survey by lead line, notwithstanding that Chart 2904
indicates that the entrance is closed by a drying reef. Inside the bottom is soft mud, depth 3m but with numerous,
almost vertical, rock heads that lie mainly on the N side of the pool so it is important not to go anything N or NW
of the entrance passage. The anchorage is restricted but offers perfect shelter for a single yacht.

Bagh na Caiplich on the E side of
Ronay about 1 mile S of the entrance
to the Sound of Flodday has offered
shelter to generations of fishermen.
The shores are steep to and the
hazards obvious, provided an
approach is made from the SE to
avoid the reefs and rocks extending 2
cables E of En an Fheidh. Hold to the
S shore to avoid the mid channel reef
and rock (dr. 0.9). Anchor in 6-9m.
Exposed to the E.

Kallin Harbour (see opposite)
Arthur Houston

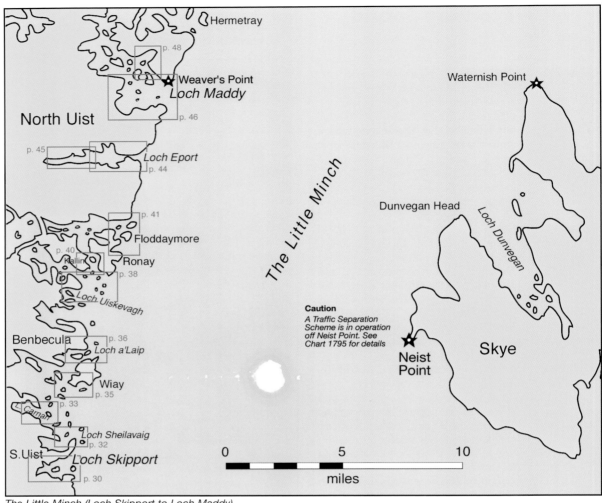

The Little Minch (Loch Skipport to Loch Maddy)

East Side of North Uist

Chart

(ii) 1795 The Little Minch
(iii) 2825 Loch Eport and Loch Maddy (Loch Madadh).
OS 18, OS 22

General

North Uist, is similar to South Uist, having steep shores and relatively high ground on its E side. The W side, particularly the NW side, is low lying and well populated. The gently rising wedge shape of two hills, South Lee (279m) and North Lee (260m) lie between Loch Eport to the S and Loch Maddy to the N. Eaval (345m) also wedge shaped and the only mountain on North Uist, lies to the S of the entrance to Loch Eport. The distance from the SE end of North Uist to Loch Maddy is about 5 miles.

The E coast of North Uist, given a reasonable berth, is free from offlying dangers. The approach to the entrance to Loch Eport is free of danger except on the S side of the entrance. Loch Maddy has however 2 islets, Madadh Gruamul (24m) (also spelt Gruamach), 4 cables S of the S side of the entrance and Madadh Mor (26m) at the S entrance. Only Madadh Mor can be passed on either hand but give its shores a good offing particularly at its N end.

Strong E'ly winds might make the seas at the entrance to Loch Eport dangerous. Loch Maddy may be entered in all weathers.

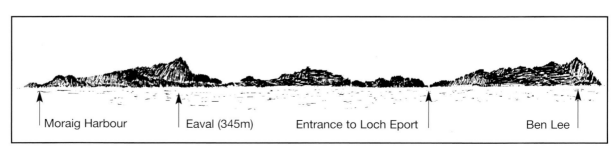

East Side of North Uist (continued)

Tides Off the E coast of North Uist run as follows
N-going stream begins —0550 Ullapool (+0215 Dover)
S-going stream begins +0035 Ullapool (—0345 Dover)
The spring rate in each direction off the salient points is 2 knots but is less between the points and the streams become weaker farther seaward.

Lights
Weaver's Point	Fl. 3s 21m 7M	N side of entrance to Loch Maddy
Neist Point	Fl. 5s 43m 16M	W point of Skye
Waternish Point	Fl. 20s 21m 8M	NW point of Skye

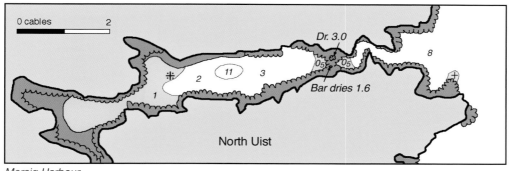

Moraig Harbour

Moraig Harbour (Bagh Moraigh)

Chart (ii) 1795 The Little Minch
(iii) 2904 Usinish to Eigneig Mhor

General A fascinating but remote landlocked anchorage (57°30.8'N 7° 09'W) at the extreme SE corner of North Uist 2.5 miles S of Loch Eport and 4 cables N of Flodday Beg. Ben Eaval is 1 mile to the NW. It would be dangerous to attempt the entrance except in favourable conditions. As the holding is poor this is an anchorage to explore in settled weather only.

Tide Const.—0040Ullapool (—0500 Dover) MHWS 4.8   MHWN 3.6   ML 2.8   MLWN 1.9   MLWS 0.7

Approach The entrance is set-in between two minor headlands. It appears to be closed because of the small isthmus projecting from the S shore thus forming a 'chicane' entrance with tight turns that could prove awkward for a vessel over 10m. The approach is deep and clear allowing you to examine the entrance without committing yourself to enter.

It is necessary to enter at or near slack HW when there will be ample depth at the 'bar' inside, and only a weak or nil stream at the narrow chicane. At mid-tide the stream can run strongly at this point and could take charge. Keep slightly towards the N shore on the first bend, then keep towards the S shore when turning W to cross the bar, leaving the large seaweed-covered rock (dr. 3m) to starboard. The middle of the bar dries 1.6m and accordingly, although more depth exists either side of the middle, it is advisable to await sufficient rise of tide before crossing the bar.

Anchorage The bottom is mainly soft mud with poor holding. There is a deep hole towards the N shore about half-way along with heavy weed on the bottom. The NW and W end of the main loch are shoal.

Moraig Harbour entrance channel with bar just visible   *Anne Mackay*

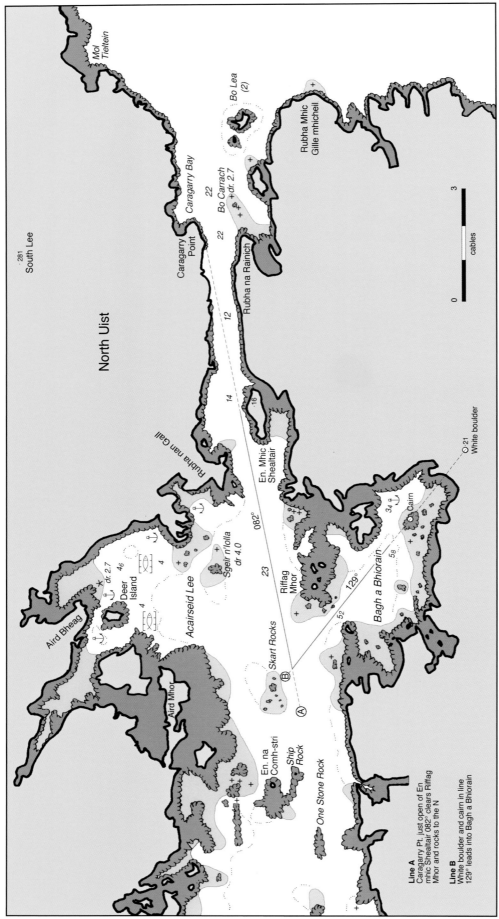

Outer Loch Eport

South Lee
·281

North Uist

Mol
Tieltein

Bo Lea
(2)

Caragarry Bay

Caragarry
Point

Bo Carrach
+ dr. 2.7

22

22

Rubha na Rainich

12

Rubha Mhic
Gille mhicheil

14

·16

Rubha nan Gall

En. Mhic
Shealtair

Aird Bheag

dr. 2.7
46

Deer
Island

4

4

Acairseid Lee

Sgeir n'Iolla
dr 4.0

23

082°

Skart Rocks

B

A

Riffag
Mhor

129°

34

Cairn

58

Bagh a Bhiorain

52

Aird Mhor

En. na
Comh-stri

Ship
Rock

One Stone Rock

21
White boulder

0   cables   3

Line A
Caragarry Pt. just open of En
mhic Shealtair 082° clears Riffag
Mhor and rocks to the N

Line B
White boulder and cairn in line
129° leads into Bagh a Bhiorain

Bagh a Bhiorain leading line
John Trythall

Loch Eport

Chart   (iii) 2825 (Plan on) Loch Eport

Tides   Const. —0040 Ullapool (—0500 Dover) MHWS 4.8   MHWN 3.6   ML 2.8   MLWN 1.9   MLWS 0.7
Tidal Streams In Loch Eport run as for Loch Uiskevagh:
In-going stream begins —0550 Ullapool (+0130 Dover)
Out-going stream begins —0020 Ullapool (—0440 Dover)
The spring rate in the narrows at the entrance is 3 knots in each direction with eddies close in shore on both sides. Once within the streams are weak in the loch. Acairseid Lee has an E going eddy during the in-going (W moving) stream. The streams run at 4 knots at springs S of Steisay and are reported to run at 10 knots with little slack water in the channel to Loch Langlass in the Inner Loch for which no directions are available.

Approach   From S or N open up the entrance and keep mid-channel to avoid, on the S side of the entrance, Bo Lea (2m) and other rocks 3 cables to the W. Maintain a mid-channel course until the loch opens out W of Eilean Mhic Shealtair at S side of inner narrows. Note clearance line 082° on plan.

Anchorage   **In Outer Loch**

Acairseid Lee on NE side of loch. Maintain a mid-channel course from outer entrance until clear of the reefs extending 1 cable W from Rubha nan Gall at N side of inner narrows. Keep the entrance of the loch a little open to pass clear S of Sgeir n'Iolla (dr 4.0m). Once clear head N for the anchorages.

E of Deer Island in 4m or, if small and manoeuvrable, NW of the island in 5m. If deciding to pass N of Deer Island note the reefs extending from the North Uist shore. Also there is an isolated rock (dr 2.7m) NE of Deer Island off the end of the reef extending SE from Aird Bheag. Alternatively anchor in 4m anywhere in the bay clear of weed. Subject to squalls.

Bagh a Bhiorain on the SE side of the loch offers sheltered anchorage. Maintain a mid-channel course from the outer entrance until the loch opens out W of Eilean Mhic Shealtair at the S side of the inner narrows. In order to avoid Riffag Mhor, comprising several low grassy islets and extensive reefs extending 4 cables W at the entrance to Bagh a Bhiorain, keep Caragarry Point on the N side of the outer entrance bearing 082° and just open N of Eilean Mhic Shealtair. This leads N of Riffag Mhor and nearby rocks. Once the entrance to the bay opens out, and before reaching Ship rock, identify a grey cairn 1.2m high on a reef in the SE corner of the bay in line with a white boulder (not always easily seen) bearing 129°. This line leads through the entrance. Keeping 30-40m from the islet to starboard while on course 129° leads safely through.
Anchor in 5m in mud or close in on the E shore NE of the cairn. In S'ly winds, E of the cairn on the centre reef can be favoured. This anchorage is less subject to squalls than Acairseid Lee.

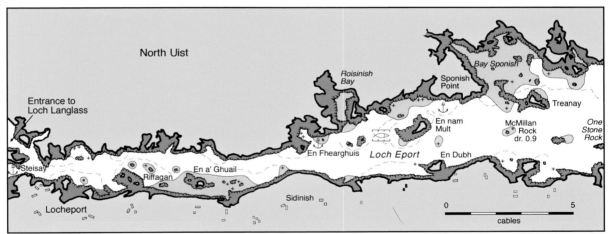

Inner Loch Eport   *NB: This plan is to a smaller scale than the plan of Outer Loch Eport opposite*

Inner Loch Eport

Approach   Maintain a mid-channel course from the outer entrance until the loch opens out W of Eilean Mhic Shealtair at the S side of the inner narrows. By keeping Caragarry Point on the N side of the outer entrance bearing 082° and just open N of Eilean Mhic Shealtair this will lead N of Riffag Mhor and clear all rocks until One Stone Rock (dr 3m) is reached.

Pass S of One Stone Rock but keep mid-channel as reefs extend from One Stone Rock and the shore to the S. Keep to the S shore until Eilean Fheargius where the loch narrows to less than 1 cable. Thereafter keep closer to the N shore until Steisay is reached. There is no chart available for the loch beyond Steisay but the head of the inner loch can be reached. Local knowledge is advisable as 1m patches exist. The OS map 18 may be useful.

Anchorage   At head of loch off the pier at Eilean a'Cairidh in 2m mud or N of Eilean a'Cairidh in 4m mud. The pier almost dries.

Facilities PO at Sidinish on the S side of the loch. Shop near the head of the loch, S side, towards the pier.

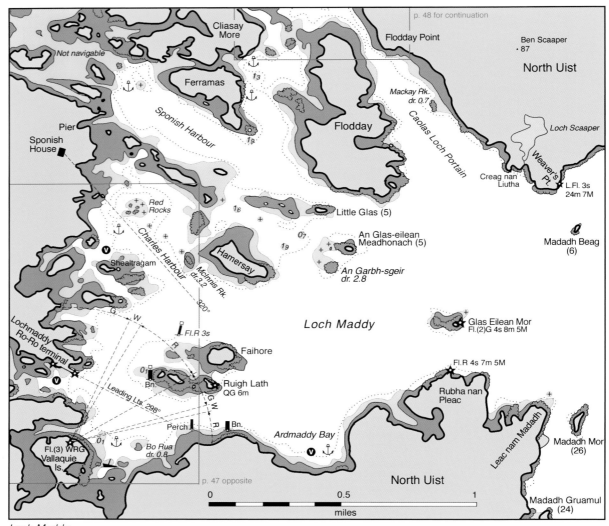

Loch Maddy

Loch Maddy (Loch Madadh)

Charts (ii) 1795 The Little Minch
(iii) 2825 Plan of Loch Maddy   OS 18

General Loch Maddy is an extensive area of sheltered water and contains many islands giving a wide choice of anchorages from which the area can be explored. Access to the main anchorage is straightforward and it is well marked and lit. Lochmaddy is one of the principal centres of population in North Uist with good services and a daily car ferry. It is about 20 miles from Loch Maddy to Loch Skipport (Wizard Pool) and 26 miles from Loch Maddy to East Loch Tarbert, Harris.

Tides Const —0040 Ullapool (—0500 Dover) MHWS 4.8 MHWN 3.6 ML 2.8 MLWN 1.9 MLWS 0.7
In-going stream begins +0555 Ullapool (+0135 Dover)
Out-going stream begins —0025 Ullapool (—0445 Dover)

Lights

Weaver's Point	Fl.3s 24m 7M	Wh Framework Twr
Vallaquie Island Sector Lt.	Fl (3). WRG. 8s 11m	Wh concrete pillar
Glas Eilean Mor	Fl (2) G 4s 8m 5M	Aluminium column
Rubha nam Pleac	Fl R 4s 7m 5M	Wh post 2 cables S of Glas Eilean Mor
Ruigh Liath, E islet	QG 6m 5M	Concrete pillar
Leading Lts bearing 298°	Front 2FG (vert). 8m 4M	Column
(on Ro-Ro Ferry Pier)	Rear Oc. G. 8s 10m 4M	Column on dolphin

Marks Madadh Gruamul (24m) 4 cables S of the S side of the entrance.
Madadh Mor (26m) at the S side of the entrance.
Madadh Beag (6m) at the N side of the entrance.

Approach

From the S When passing W of Madadh Mor note the submerged rock 0.5 cable N of Leac nam Madadh. Passing E of Madadh Mor note reefs extend N from it. Pass S of Glas Eilean at the entrance to the loch and Ruigh Liath if making for the moorings in the vicinity of Lochmaddy Ro-Ro Terminal.(VHF Ch 16 and 12 'Loch Maddy Harbour')

From the N Pass Madadh Beag on either hand and if heading for the moorings near the Ro-Ro Terminal pass at least 1 cable W and NW of Glas Eilean Mor and leave an Glais-eilean Meadhonach and An Gairbh-sgeir (dr 2.8m) at least 1 cable to starboard. The Ro-Ro Terminal may be approached either S or N of Ruigh Liath and Faihore. Give both a wide berth as reefs extend in all directions and note the white beacon W of Ruigh Liath, and R pole with light Fl R 3s 4M, NW of Faihore, both of which are shown on the plan.

Note: In strong winds, with wind against tide, the seas at the entrance may be very bad, particularly off Weavers Point and Leac nam Madadh. It may be better in such circumstances to enter the loch in mid-channel.

Anchorage

Near the Ro-Ro terminal Anchor SW and well clear of the pier. Note the reef (dr 1.7m) nearby. There are **5 visitors moorings**, 2 W of the Ro-Ro pier and 3 in the next bay to the W. Rocks in the W bay are marked by an E Cardinal buoy and by a perch with topmark. **Alternatively** tie up to the N (inner) side of the pier as near to the sheds as depth will allow with lines ashore to keep off the pier. Keep clear of the ferry when it is manoeuvring at the round-head.

Vallaquie 4 cables SE of the Ro-Ro Terminal. Easy to approach but exposed to the N. Do not approach at HW as the wreck in the S section of the bay covers. In settled weather anchor N of the wreck. To obtain shelter from the swell pass close W of the wreck and proceed to the middle of the bay which shoals gently. Soft mud. Note Weaver's Point in line with the SE side of Ruigh Liath leads N of Bogha Rua.

Ardmaddy Bay (Bagh Aird nam Madadh) Situated just inside the S entrance to the loch this bay provides excellent anchorage. Anchor in 3 to 5m but preferably in the SE corner where no swell is felt even in E'ly winds. Squally in SW winds. Exposed to the NE. **Two visitors moorings**.

Charles Harbour. Entering, keep mid-channel heading 320° for Sponish House, a conspicuous 3 storey building, with McInnis Rock (dr 3.2m) 1 cable W of Hamersay on the starboard hand and the extensive reefs off Shealtragam (dr 2.6m) to port. Entering before half

Lochmaddy Harbour & anchorages

tide allows the reefs and rocks to be seen. At any state of the tide the safe channel is 1 cable wide. Anchor in 6 or 8m mud, very soft in places, E of Eilean Fear Vallay. If moving about in this area beware of Red Rock, an extensive reef which just dries about 1 cable NE of Eilean Fear Vallay.

Oronsay. This small enclosed area NW of Oronsay is well sheltered but with little or no room to anchor. It is occupied by moorings of local boats. Do not tie up to local boats without permission. Further in just clear of the moorings it is very soft mud and yachts sink in without listing. The pier with 2m at HW Neaps and which dries out may be laid alongside temporarily whilst shopping or during short visits ashore. Water at pier. Enter from Charles Harbour passing SE then SW of Eilean Fear Vallay. Follow the Uist shore when entering the narrow channel, with less than 2m at LW, N of Oronsay. **Two visitors moorings** E of Oronsay.

Sponish Harbour. Approach between Flodday and Little Glas. From the S pass to the E and N well clear of An Glas-eilean Meadhonach and An Gairbh-sgeir (dr 3.2m) with their adjoining reefs and rocks. Proceeding into the harbour keep in the centre of the channel between Ferramas and islets to the S. Anchor anywhere in suitable depth when S to SW of Ferramas. Take care to avoid the approaches to the pier and the submerged rock 1c W of Ferramas. The extension to the pier at the NW head of Sponish Harbour may offer shelter in severe conditions.

Pool W of Flodday. More shelter is provided anchoring in 7m on the E side of Ferramas or nearby in 6m at the inlet between Ferramas and Cliasay Mor. Note the reefs extending half way into the pool from Flodday and a shoal patch (1.3m) 100m E of the NE corner of Ferramas. This area must be approached from the S.

Facilities

Shops (EC Wednesday) at Lochmaddy and supermarket at Sollas. PO, tel. bank, hotel. Water at pier (hose from storeman). Petrol and diesel from garage. Calor gas - phone 01876 500202. Car Ferry daily to Uig, Skye and Tarbert, Harris. Bus to airport on Benbecula and Sollas. Tourist Information Centre tel. 01878 700286.

Interest

Excellent Visitor Centre. Hire a car or taxi and visit the many beautiful beaches to the W such as Clachan Sands, or the many interesting archaeological sites in North Uist or Benbecula. In settled conditions or in suitable weather anchor in the bay N of Creag nan Luitha off the pebble beach. Row ashore and fish in **Loch Scaaper**, a fresh water loch just above beach level. Or climb Ben Scaaper for a panoramic view of Loch Maddy.

Loch Portain

General

This secluded loch forms the NE arm of Loch Maddy and this description should be read in conjunction with those on the previous two pages. The loch provides good shelter although in parts the mud is soft and care is worth taking to obtain good holding.

Approach

Pass mid-channel straight through Caolas Loch Portain, NE of Flodday. Just before Rubha nan Gall turn to port to keep a cable off the point. Turn to starboard and enter Loch Portain only when its S shore opens. Pass S of the islet and anchor in 2 or 3m in mud, but not further in than 2 cables.

Anchorage

Holding is reported as good in thick grey mud particularly in mid-channel 0.5c ESE of the islet, so it is worthwhile seeking this as certain areas are reported as poor.

Facilities

Tel. - the box is not easily found. It is behind the white house on the right between the slip and the main road.

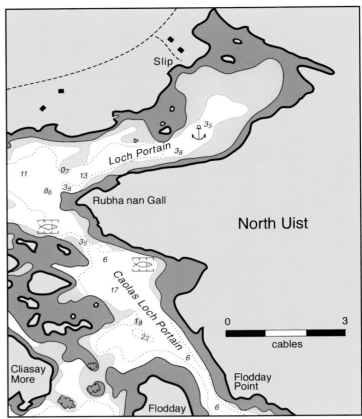

Loch Portain

Sound of Harris

Charts

(iii) 2802 Sound of Harris. **A new chart was published in July 2008 superseding the previous chart, 2642. The new chart is conventionally aligned to the meridian and is essential for navigating the Sound.**

Approaching from W
(i) 2721 St Kilda to Butt of Lewis (general approach information)
(iii) 2841 Loch Maddy to Loch Resort (including Sound of Harris)
Approaching from E
(ii) 1795 The Little Minch (general approach information)
OS map 18

General

The Sound of Harris which separates the largest island of the Outer Hebrides, Lewis and Harris from North Uist, is about 8 to 9 miles running SE to NW and has many reef and rock hazards. When considering a passage either W'wards or E'wards there is a choice of channels. The **Stanton Channel** and to a lesser extent the **Leverburgh Channel,** both between Ensay and South Harris, are the main channels through the Sound of Harris and provide better depths than the **Cope Passage** which passes between the Hermetray and Groay groups of islands at the SE entrance to the Sound and between Berneray and Killegray at the NW entrance. Though well buoyed and lit the Cope Passage is essentially a fair weather channel for vessels drawing no more than 2m. Since it was buoyed in 2007, the **Stanton Channel** is generally the route preferred by most vessels passing through the Sound. For directions for both channels see pp. 58-59 (Stanton) & 54-55 (Cope).

Two groups of islands and islets, the Hermetray and Groay groups, are situated at the SE side of the Sound. The former, lying close to the coast of North Uist, offers a number of anchorages and provides a base from which to explore the intricate channels between North Uist and Berneray.

The central area of the Sound is occupied by three larger islands, Berneray, Killegray and Ensay. The tide is strongest in the channels between these islands. In **Caolas Skaari** between Ensay and Killegray, the spring rate achieves 5 knots and as the channel is narrow, with many reefs, rocks and shoal patches on either hand, It is dangerous and cannot be recommended.

The introduction of a **vehicle ferry service** between Leverburgh on South Harris and a terminal at the causeway between Berneray and North Uist has required the positioning of perches and buoys to mark the intricate route across the Sound. These must be distinguished from the buoys marking the Cope Passage. Provided the buoys and perches marking the ferry route are identified the approach from the Cope Passage to the Bays Loch is greatly simplified. (see pp. 54 & 56)

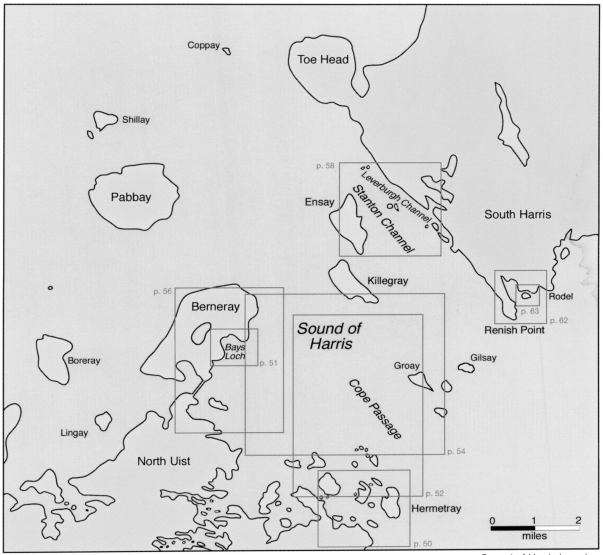

Sound of Harris key plan

Sound of Harris (continued)

The NW entrance to the Sound is readily recognised by the islands of Pabbay and Shillay to the W and by Coppay and Toe Head on South Harris to the N. Approaching from the W it should be entered between Shillay and Coppay.

Returning from W and unsure if entry to the Sound of Harris over the Cope Channel bar may be safely navigated, proceeding to the Stanton Channel or seeking shelter in the lee of Pabbay, taking into account the shoal patches, may provide a suitable alternative

Tides

In the Sound of Harris
Like all bodies of water those in and around the Sound of Harris are subject to daily (diurnal) as well as twice daily (semi-diurnal) gravitational influences from both the moon and the sun. The Sound responds to these influences differently at spring tides as compared to neap tides in what might be considered interesting ways, if not necessarily complex. The patterns of tidal behaviour are not the same in all parts of the Sound. Tidal information is given within each section pertaining to that part of the Sound being dealt with.

Basically the in-coming flood stream enters the Sound at the NW entrance and runs all the way through to the Little Minch where It joins the NE going flood.

Off the SE entrance to the Sound the streams change very quickly at the turn of the tide. In the vicinity of the SE entrance to the Sound the streams begin up to 2.5 hours later than they do to the S of the Sound.

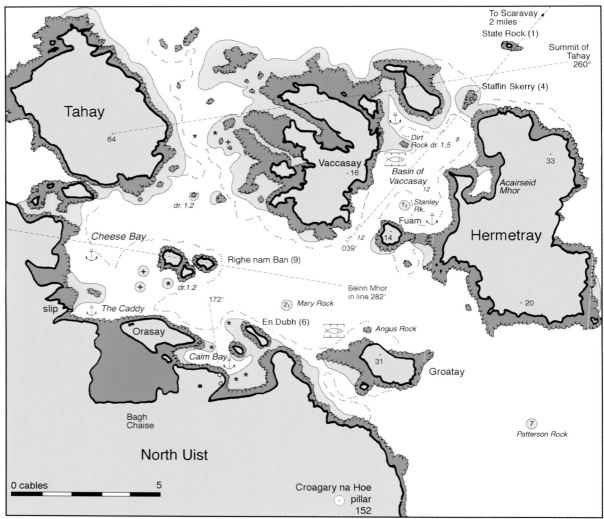

Hermetray, Vaccasay and North Uist anchorages

Hermetray Group of Islands

Chart   (iii) 2802 Sound of Harris
            OS18

General   The Hermetray Group of Islands are situated at the SE entrance to the Sound of Harris. They are within the Sound close N of North Uist about 6 miles from Lochmaddy. Vaccasay Basin between Hermetray and Vaccasay offers the best, if rather solitary, shelter. Calm Bay on North Uist is nearer habitation and is said to be sheltered from all winds. Opsay basin, a mile N from Vaccasay Basin, is entered from the E through the Grey Horse Channel (see plan and text pp. 52 & 53). It is completely surrounded by low islets and reefs and is open to the sky and wind.

Tides   Const. —0040 Ullapool (—0500 Dover) Range as for Leverburgh (see p. 60)
            Among the islands of Hermetray group;
            NW going stream begins —0535 Ullapool (+0230 Dover)
            SE going stream begins +0035 Ullapool (—0345 Dover)
            The spring rate in the narrower parts of the channels may be as much as 3 knots in each direction.

Approach   **From S** make for the middle of Hermetray. In heavy swell keep clear of Patterson Rock, with 7m over it, between Leac na Hoe, North Uist and Hermetray. Then alter course to pass mid way between Groatay and Hermetray. Once the most E'ly islet of the Righe nam Ban group comes under Beinn Mhor, a course of 282° will clear Angus Rock and Mary Rock.

            From N either pass E of Hermetray and then approach as from the S or, if the visibility is good, steer from the Fairway Lt buoy RW (LFl 10s) marking the entrance to the Cope Passage on a course of 260° to the summit of Tahay passing 1 cable N of Greanem (see plan p. 52). Alter course to pass mid-way between State Rock and Staffin Skerry. The Basin of Vaccasay is entered passing W of Staffin Skerry.

            Clearance bearing When passing through Vaccasay Basin keep Staffin Skerry in line astern with the SE right hand edge of Scaravay, the S'most island of the Groay group, bearing 039° and distant 2 miles. This clears both Dirt Rock and Stanley Rock.

Anchorage **Vaccasay Basin**

Between Hermetray and Vaccasay, the basin may be entered W of Fuam or from the N (see opposite). Passage between Fuam and Hermetray should not be attempted. Anchor in the bay NE of Fuam but note Stanley Rock N of Fuam with 1.8m over it. There is extensive fish farming in this area. Proceed through the basin with caution.

The **NW corner of the basin** in suitable depths and conditions offers good anchorage. Note Dirt Rock, dr. 1.5m, 0.5 cable off Vaccasay.

Acairseid Mhor an inlet 0.5 cable wide on NW side of Hermetray should be entered mid-channel as rocky shelves extend from both sides. Uncomfortable in N'ly winds and poor holding with thick weed. The innermost part is reported free from weed but is suitable only for very small yachts which would need to moor. Water at spring close to the shore on E side of island.

Cheese Bay (North Uist shore) Although not a snug anchorage this bay provides a large area of reasonable depth for anchoring in good holding, mud.

Calm Bay (Bagh Chaise, North Uist shore)
Noting the position of Mary Rock with 2.1m in over it, alter to port but give En Dubh a wide berth to avoid the drying rock WNW of the island, as the marks leading clear of these and shown on the plan are reported (2008) as obscured or missing. Keep in the the eastern 1/3 of the entrance passage to avoid the drying reef which extends from Orosay more than halfway across the entrance. Anchor in 2-3m between the islet SW of Eilean Dubh and the shore where the leading marks are shown; mud with shells. (Note: If the marks are visible, keep to the E of the leading line when in the entrance as it leads very close to the drying reef.)

The Caddy (North Uist shore)
Anchor close NW of Orasay off the slipway in 3-4m but keep clear of fairway used by local vessels. Subject to weed. Approach S of Righe nam Ban.

Hermetray group

Jane Routh

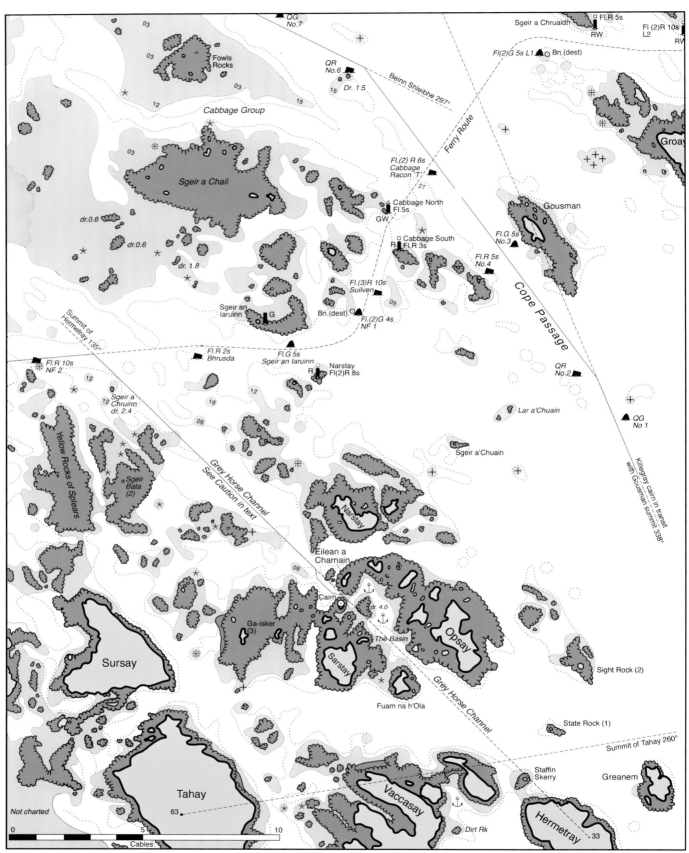

Sound of Harris, Grey Horse Channel

Opsay Basin

General This basin lies between the low lying islets and extensive reefs at the E end of the Grey Horse Channel marked by a cairn.

Approach **From Vaccasay Basin** pass W of Staffin Skerry heading towards Opsay. Alter course to make a mid-channel approach as Grey Horse Channel opens out passing N of Fuam na h'Ola.

From N or E From Fairway Lt buoy RW (LFl 10s) head to pass between Sight Rock and State Rock till Grey Horse Channel opens. Pass N of Fuam na h'Ola. If in doubt follow course 260° to summit of Tahay (see plan opposite) passing 1 cable N of Greanem then between Staffin Skerry and State Rock before altering course as the Grey Horse Channel opens out.

Anchorage At outer entrance keep mid-channel to avoid reefs extending 1 cable SW from Opsay. The entrance is not narrow but be sure to turn into the basin only when clear of extending reefs on either hand. Anchor E of the drying reef NE of Sarstay in 6m. Some weed. Further N a bottom of mud and shells can be found in 3-4m. The rocks E and S of the cairn (The Grey Horse) dry about 4m.

Grey Horse Channel

General The Grey Horse Channel runs between Hermetray and Greanem to Opsay Basin where it narrows between many islets. It continues NW through a narrow passage N of the Cairn and finds its way amidst shoals and rocks to Bays Loch, Berneray. Because there is now a well marked ferry route from the Cope Passage to the Bays Loch (see pp. 54-56) there is now no requirement even to consider using the NW section of the Grey Horse Channel except to prove to oneself that it can be done! However the following directions, when used with Chart 2802 and extreme caution, may be of interest.

Directions The NW section of the Grey Horse Channel N'wards from Opsay Basin should only be attempted in clear settled weather and with a rising tide, preferably beginning at LW so that some of the dangers are visible. However awaiting the rise of tide may delay access to Bays Loch from the ferry route (see p. 57).

From Opsay Basin pass N of the Grey Horse ("Cairn" on chart) and keep the highest part of Hermetray astern over the passage N of the Grey Horse on a bearing of 135°. For the first cable or so keep a little S of this line until clear of drying rocks NW of Eilean a'Charnain. After a mile Sgeir a'Chruinn (dr 2.4m) is left to port. This rock may show white when covered at half tide. After this point the flood tide sets strongly to the SW and must be allowed for when joining the ferry route to Berneray (see plans and text on pp. 52, 54 & 56).

Caution Remember that although the plan opposite shows large areas of reefs or rocks which dry many of these reefs will not show, and depths in the channel itself may vary considerably.

Stanton Channel looking NW towards Saghay More (centre left) and Kyles Lodge (pp. 58 & 59)   *Charles Tait*

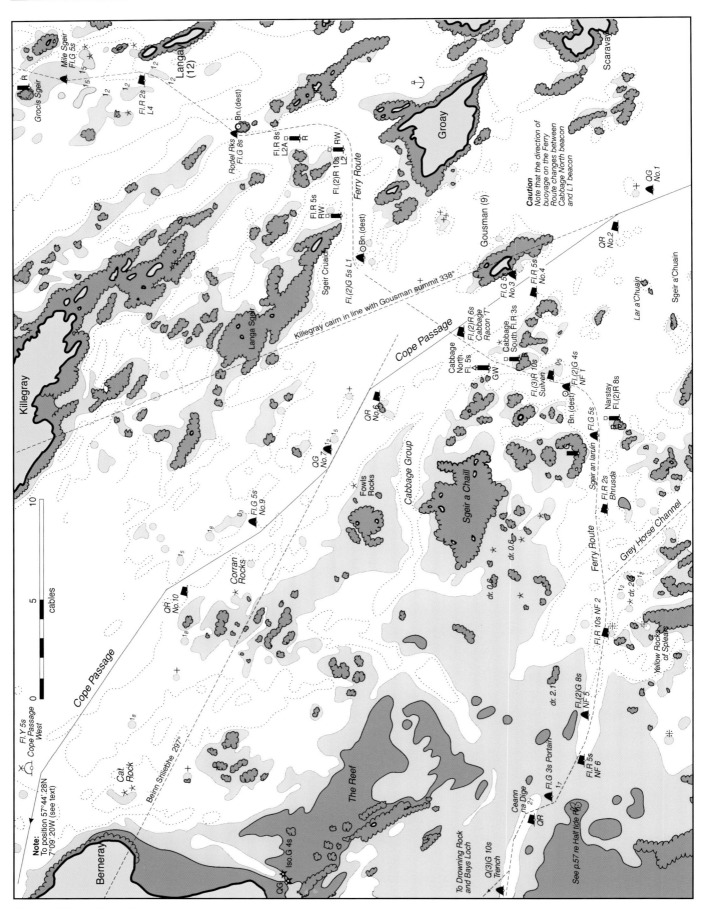

Sound of Harris, Cope Passage

Cope Passage

Chart
(iii) 2802 Sound of Harris

General
The passage was originally laid by Stanley Cope in 1957 for shallow draft Army vessels supplying the base at St Kilda, so as to avoid the strong tidal streams of the Stanton Channel. From its SE entrance a stable channel, with weak streams and well marked by lit buoys, leads NW between isolated rocks to a position NE of Berneray, marked by a special buoy. Beyond this buoy the route, which is unmarked, passes across the WSW end of a shifting sand bar. **Unless one has recent local knowledge, it should only be used in moderate weather by craft drawing no more than 2m.**

Lights
From SE to NW *(Note buoys No 5 and No 8 were permanently removed in 2007)*

Fairway buoy (57° 40'.35N 7° 02'.15W)	LFl 10s	RW spherical buoy
No 1 (SE entrance to Cope Passage)	QG	Green conical buoy
No 2 (SE entrance to Cope Passage)	QR	Red can buoy
No 3 (SW of Gousman)	Fl G 5s	Green conical buoy
No 4 (SW of Gousman)	Fl R 5s	Red can buoy
Cabbage (NW of Gousman)	Fl (2) R 6s Racon (T)	Red can buoy
No 6 (NE of Cabbage Group)	QR	Red can buoy
No 7 (N of Cabbage Group)	QG	Green conical buoy
No 9 (E of Corran Rocks)	Fl G 5s	Green conical buoy
No 10 (NNE of Corran Rocks)	QR	Red can buoy
Cope Passage West (NE of Berneray)	Fl Y 5s	Yellow spherical buoy with 'X' topmark

(See Caution and Directions below concerning the bar between Berneray and Killegray, also note on plan)

Tides
Constant: —0040 Ullapool (—0500 Dover) MHWS 4.7   MHWN 3.5   ML 2.7   MLWN 1.8   MLWS 0.6
Tidal streams seldom exceed one knot; it is believed that **rates are generally 0.5 knots or less.**
NB. Since 1974 the Admiralty Pilot has given specific stream data 'on the bar NE of Berneray', as repeated in previous editions of this pilot. This was an editorial error, as the data was in fact for a quite different location.

Caution
Based on information in the Admiralty Pilot
A bar, consisting of loose shifting sand, extends N from Berneray and then E to Killegray. Chart 2802 shows the approximate position and form of this bar in 2004. The NW part of the main shoal bank had a steep slope on its seaward side and during surveys across the bar, in freshening onshore winds, heavy breakers were suddenly encountered close seaward of this steep slope. These had developed within 40 minutes. Such breakers would be dangerous, particularly as they might not be seen from seaward until craft are upon them.

The precise track given in the directions below leads through a channel close to the Berneray coast. Available data and reports indicate that this channel has been reasonably stable. To allow for the uncertainty of shifting sands, it is recommended that the passage should not be taken with less height of tide than the draught of the craft. **Extreme caution is required and craft should not attempt passage over the bar in adverse weather conditions.** The bar should only be approached in conditions such that the craft could readily reverse its course and implement an alternative passage plan.

Directions
For Passage from SE to NW
It should be noted that the general direction of buoyage for the Sound of Harris is NW. Thus when approaching the Cope Passage from SE, all red can buoys must be left to port and all green conical buoys to starboard. The best track is made by passing all these lateral marks at a distance of 0.5c. If leaving the Cope Passage to follow the Ferry route, note that the local direction of buoyage on the Ferry route changes at the point where it crosses the Cope Passage (see plan opposite). Care is needed not to confuse the lighted marks on these two routes, particularly at night or in reduced visibility.

The Fairway RW buoy (LFl 10s), in position 57° 40'.35N 7° 02'.15W, marks the SE entrance to Cope Passage. The buoy lies on a bearing of 338° with the conspicuous cairn on Killegray in line with the summit of Gousman. Follow this charted track, passing SW of No 1 G buoy and NE of No 2 R buoy. When abeam No 2 R buoy, alter course to pass midway between No 3 G and No 4 R buoys, keeping well clear of the reefs which extend almost 3 cables SE from Gousman. The Cabbage R buoy marks the crossing of the Ferry route and the Cope Passage, being a port-hand mark for both. Follow the marked channel NW, past No 6 R buoy, No 7 G buoy, No 9 G buoy and then No 10 R buoy, the last of the lateral marks.

Continue NW, so as to pass 0.5c SSW of Cope Passage West Y spherical buoy. This special buoy marks both the NW end of the stable buoyed channel and the SE side of the shifting sand bar, which has to be crossed in the final mile of the passage. From this position 0.5c SSW of the buoy, the track leads WNW for a distance of 6c to position 57°44'.28N 7°09'.20W where it turns NNW to position 57°45.0N 7°10'.0W, clear of the bar. Continue NNW to the Atlantic, noting The Reef, extending more than 2c E of Pabbay, and Halo Rock (LD 3.7) to starboard. **Caution**: this precise track across the shifting bar has been derived from 2004 survey data. Depths should be observed frequently and compared to those charted as a precaution against subsequent changes.

For Passage from NW to SE
As for SE to NW but in reverse. If in any doubt about the conditions at the bar N of Berneray use either of the main channels, Stanton or Leverburgh, both at the NE side of the Sound of Harris (see pp. 58 & 59).

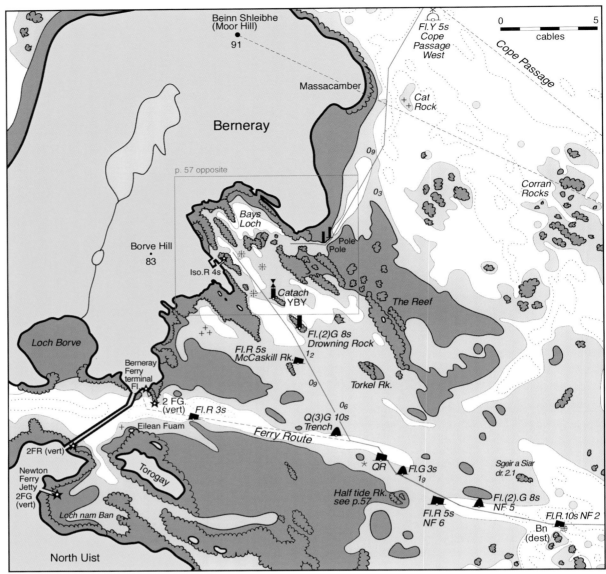

Approaches to Bays Loch, Berneray

Bays Loch, Berneray

Chart (iii) 2802 Sound of Harris

General Berneray, well within the Sound of Harris, is close N of the N'most extremity of North Uist. The W and N coasts have extensive sand dunes. Its E side has an anchorage in Bays Loch which can be approached either by following the ferry route or by the Reef Channel (see opposite) but, as both approaches have some soundings of well under a metre, an adequate rise of tide is needed. The harbour on the S side of Bays Loch allows entry at most states of the tide.

Tides Constant: —0046 Ullapool (—0506 Dover) MHWS 4.7 MHWN 3.6 ML 2.7 MLWN 1.9 MLWS 0.7
The tidal flow is likely to be complex on the E and S side of Berneray and the wind strength and direction is likely to influence its strength and direction. The direction of flow is liable to be across the channels. At the Reef Channel the rate of flow in either direction is 4 knots springs.

Lights

At the Reef Channel
N pole beacon   Unlit
S pole beacon   Unlit

Approach to Harbour from Ferry route
McCaskill Rock   Fl.R 5s   R buoy
Drowning Rock   Fl.(2)G 8s 2m 2M Perch

At Berneray Harbour
Outer breakwater   Iso R.4s 6m 4M

At Berneray Ferry Terminal
Head of ferry slip   Fl
End of breakwater 2FG(vert) 6m 3M
SE of breakwater   Fl.R 3s R can buoy

Newton Jetty, North Uist
End of jetty   2 FG(vert) 6m 3M

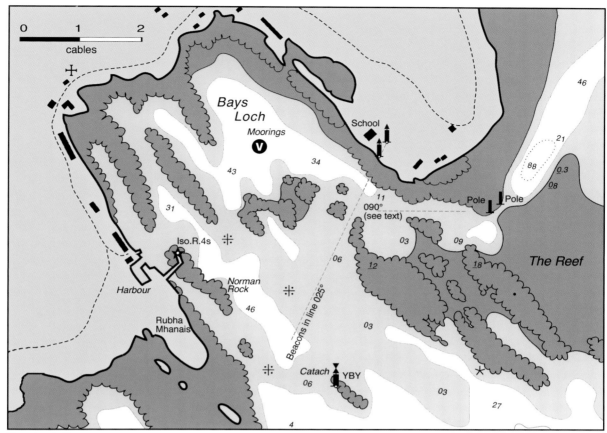

Bays Loch, Berneray

Approach   **The Ferry Route** This straightforward approach is from Cope Passage by following the ferry route but do not leave the ferry route until the half tide rock is covered. (see plan on p. 56)

If proceeding NW in the Cope Passage with the intention of joining the Ferry Route maintain a N'ly course after passing R buoy No.4 until the Cabbage North perch on the ferry route bears less than 240°, and the perch on Cabbage South is identified. This turning point is marked by a R buoy, 'Cabbage', Fl.(2)R 6s, Racon 'T' (see plan on p. 54). Alter course to port and follow the ferry route precisely until just before the Trench buoy is reached; then alter course to leave the Trench buoy to port and Drowning Rock and Catach, both marked by perches, to starboard during the final approach either to the Harbour or to the anchorage in the NW corner of the loch.

Crossing Bays Loch the transit triangles on the NE shore on a bearing of 025° must be used. If proceeding S'wards and making for the harbour give the breakwater a wide berth of at least 50m.

The Reef Channel The alternative approach to Bays Loch is through the extremely narrow 15–20m wide channel between the reef extending E'wards from the Berneray shore and the area of rocks known as 'The Reef'. Firstly, when leaving the Cope Passage to approach The Reef Channel, pass close to the Cope Passage West buoy and hold to the Berneray shore to avoid Cat Rock. Thereafter make for the two tall wood piles which resemble telephone poles which stand on the E extremity of the reef on the Berneray side of the channel (see photograph p. 60). The poles must be left to starboard and passed within 5-7m. Do not alter to starboard immediately after passing the S'most pole but alter round gradually to bring that pole on a line astern on a distant 6 mile transit of 090° with Dunaarin (a conspic. island the shape of a small Ailsa Craig). This leading line will lead clear of shoal water on either side until making a turn towards the N area of Bays Loch. Continue to maintain a close watch for shoal water (see plan)

Anchorage   **In the N area of the loch** in 4m. There are three visitors moorings.

The Harbour has 1.3m at LW. The immediate approaches NW of Norman Rock may dry. The entrance is narrow and on entry a sharp turn to port is required.

Loch nam Ban On N Uist, S of Berneray, is favourably reported as an anchorage, especially at neaps. Anchor as far in as soundings and state of tide permit, going to SE of jetty at neaps. Beware drying reef off E point of entrance, and drying rocks in middle of the bay.

Facilities   Water hose, toilets, shower and telephone at Berneray Harbour. Diesel (key card needed, see p. 5). Post Office and small shop in village on NW side of Bays Loch. Licensed stores and tearoom at Ardmaree, close to ferry terminal. Calor gas up the Borve road on the left. Bus routes to North Uist and southwards. Youth Hostel on E point of Bays Loch.

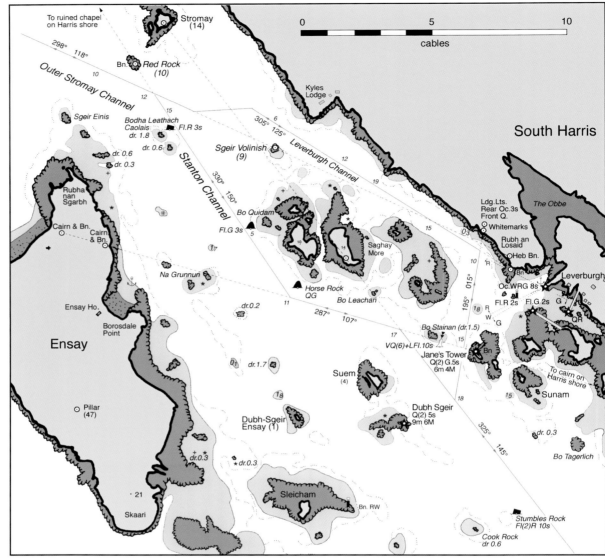

Sound of Harris, Stanton and Leverburgh channels

Stanton Channel

Chart

(iii) 2802 Sound of Harris

General

The main channel through the Sound of Harris is the Stanton Channel. Although nowhere in the channel is the width of safe water less than 1.5 cables, **the dangers on either side and the need to cross tidal streams demand that the track shown and transits given are carefully followed**. Some of the transits, which were formerly the prime navigational aids before the channel was buoyed, are shown on the chart and the above plan to provide a degree of guidance in clear weather. If using GPS in poor visibility it is essential to monitor the cross-track error. An alternative route through the Sound is the Leverburgh Channel (see opposite) which passes NW of Jane's Tower but in places it is restricted in width to little over half a cable and it is necessary to follow the transits carefully. Both channels join up with the Outer Stromay Channel between Ensay and Stromay.

Lights & buoys

Dubh Sgeir Beacon	Q(2) 5s 9m 6M	Red concrete Twr. with black bands
Jane's Tower Beacon	Q(2) G.5s 6m 4M	Stone pedestal with cream and green bands
		Sector obscured 273° - 318° (45°)
Stumbles Rock	Fl.(2)R.10s	Red can buoy
Bo Stainan	VQ(6)+LFl.10s	S Cardinal buoy
Horse Rock	QG	Green conical buoy
Bo Quidam	Fl.G 3s	Green conical buoy
Bodha Leathach Caolais	Fl.R 3s	Red can buoy
Red Rock	*Planned to be lit*	Green Lattice beacon (see above)
Colasgeir	Fl.(2)R 8s	Red can buoy

Red Rock Beacon

Sgeir Volinish Beacon (Red)

Stanton Channel (continued)

Tides **Constant:** —0040 Ullapool (—0500 Dover)   MHWS 4.6   MHWN 3.5   MTL 2.6   MLWN 1.9   MLWS 0.6

In the channels between Ensay and Harris, including the Stanton Channel and Leverburgh Channels, the streams are remarkable. The SE-going stream begins +0545 Ullapool (+0125 Dover) and the NW-going stream begins —0025 Ullapool (—0445 Dover). This is the norm. However during the summer at neaps it has been observed that the SE-going stream runs during the day and the NW-going stream at night. The spring rate S of Saghay More is 4 knots.

Passage from SE to NW (from the Minches to the Atlantic)

Approach Enter the Sound from the Minches between Renish Point, S Harris and Dun-aarin, the most E'ly of the Groay group of islands and readily identified by its height (26m) and angular profile. In wind against tide conditions give Renish Point a good offing. Make for the R buoy marking the Stumbles Rock or if it cannot be made out, head between Jane's Tower and the beacon on Dubh Sgeir. Jane's Tower is under the peak of Chaipaval at the NW point of the Sound and Dubh Sgeir beacon resembles a disused lighthouse and is the more conspicuous having open water behind it. The Stumbles R buoy must be left to port.

Directions From the Stumbles R buoy pass between Jane's Tower and the beacon on Dubh Sgeir on a course of 325° towards the stone beacon on Saghay More. When past Suem alter towards the G buoy SW of Horse Rock. Note that the transit of 287° on the plan may not be recognised as the lower cairn on Ensay has been reported as inconspic. The tidal streams may be strong here (see Caution above).

When the Horse Rock G buoy is abeam alter to starboard towards the Red Rock lattice beacon leaving the G buoy W of Bo Quidam to starboard and the R buoy E of Bodha Leathach Caolais to port. At a distance of 1 cable from the Red Rock beacon alter to a course of 298° to pass NW'wards out through the Outer Stromay Channel leaving the R buoy marking Colasgeir (dr 2.4m) close to port. Doing so will avoid rocks (dr 0.3m) lying 5c ENE of Colasgeir.

Passage from NW to SE (from the Atlantic to the Minches)

Approach **From N & NW** Beinn a'Charnain on Pabbay is conspicuous as is Chaipaval on Harris. Pass to the W of Coppay and at least 1 mile to the S before identifying the Colasgeir R buoy and lining up with the Outer Stromay Channel. **From W** it is best to pass through the **Sound of Shillay** to approach the Outer Stromay Channel.

If the Colasgeir R buoy is difficult to see, keeping the lattice beacon on Red Rock in line with the lattice beacon on Sgeir Volinish 122° will avoid any dangers until close enough to identify the buoy and pick up the 118° transit bearing given below and on the plan.

Directions Leaving the Colasgeir R buoy to starboard enter the Outer Stromay Channel on a bearing of 118° using the transit of the Heb Beacon on Rubh 'an Losaid in line with Sgeir Volinish Beacon. Maintain this course, passing S of Red Rock Beacon, until 1 cable beyond it before turning to starboard on to a course of 150°. Leave the R buoy marking Bodha Leathach Caolais to starboard and follow the track on the plan leaving both the G buoy W of Bo Quidam and the second G buoy SW of Horse Rock to port. Avoid straying towards the Na Grunnun group of rocks.

After passing the Horse Rock buoy course can be altered to pass between Suem and the S cardinal buoy marking Bo Stainan. Thereafter proceed to pass E of the Stumbles Rock R buoy.

Anchorage **Ensay** in bay on NE side, off the large house. Approach from NW is best from the direction of Sgeir Volinish noting carefully the hazards on either hand. **Alternatively** from the SE at Stumbles Rock R buoy (in conditions of good visibility) pass S of Dubh Sgeir Ensay and on a course of 331° keeping the S tangent of the Harris shore below the slopes of Chaipaval just open of the N tangent of Ensay, the hazards are cleared on either hand. Maintain this course passing between the reefs off Borosdale Point and those round Na Grunnan. Do not turn into anchorage until the house bears 225°. The anchorage is sheltered from E through S to NW. Note the reefs extending from either side of the bay especially from the E. (see photograph p. 60)

Leverburgh Channel

Directions **From SE to NW** approach as described for the Stanton channel towards the stone beacon on Saghay More on a course of 325°. Alter course to starboard just before Jane's Tower and the beacon on Dubh Sgeir are abeam, when the white transit marks NW of Rubh'an Losaid are in line bearing 015°. Keep on this transit until fairly close to the shore then turn to port to bring a small iron beacon on the shore (below the Heb beacon) in line with the Leverburgh pierhead astern bearing 125°. Steer 305° to pass N of the red lattice beacon on Sgeir Volinish. After passing Sgeir Volinish steer to pass S of the lattice beacon on Red Rock and join the Outer Stromay channel then follow the Directions for the SE to NW passage. **Caution;** In poor or marginal visibility the transits may be difficult to identify.

From NW to SE approach and follow the Outer Stromay channel as described above for the Stanton channel but after passing 1c S of the Red Rock beacon steer a course of 118° until 3c from Sgeir Volinish. Now head for Kyles Lodge on the Harris shore and turn to starboard when the small iron beacon and Leverburgh pierhead described above are in line 125°. Turn to starboard again only when the white transit marks on the Harris shore can be brought to bear 015° astern. Pass W of Jane's Tower on this transit on a heading of 195°. Once between the beacon on Dubh Sgeir and Jane's Tower, turn to port and steer to leave the Stumbles Rock R buoy to starboard.

Leverburgh

Tides   **Constant:** —0040 Ullapool (—0500 Dover) MHWS 4.6   MHWN 3.5   MTL 2.6   MLWN 1.9   MLWS 0.6

Lights
Leverburgh Pier head	Oc WRG 8s 5m 2M	Sectors G305°-059° (114°) W059°-066° (7°), R066°-125° (59°)
Leverburgh leading Lts.	Front: Q 10m 4M	Wh. mast
(bearing 015°)	Rear: Oc 3s 12m 4M	Wh. plinth
Leverburgh reef	Fl R 2s	R&W perch SW of Leverburgh pier
Outer breakwater	Fl.G 2s 5m 3M	
Inner breakwater	QR 5m 3M	

Approach   As described for the Leverburgh Channel but leave the transit (white marks on Rubh'an Losaid in line 015°) when the R&W perch (Fl R 2s) is in line with the head of the pier (Oc WRG 8s 5m 2M). Turn towards the pier and leave the perch to port. **Alternatively**, with care and avoiding the 1.5m patch, pass W of Sunam between it and Eilean na Cloicheig. Once through the passage do not make for the area of the pier until the beacon on Dubh Sgeir and Jane's Tower are in line astern. At night the pierhead light may not be picked out due to the glare of the sodium lights nearby.

Facilities   Shop, PO, tel, petrol and road diesel at shop, Calor gas, water at pier. Diesel (key card needed, see p. 5). Craft shop. Bank (Thursday only), Car hire. Tearoom/Restaurant at craft shop. Vehicle ferry service to Berneray and N Uist.

Anchorage   Anchor either side of the pier and clear of moorings but keep clear of the ferry turning area. There are two breakwaters S and SE of the pierhead giving protection to the ferry berth and small craft moorings.

Carminish Bay on the SE side of Carminish Peninsula, Harris, 2 miles NW of Renish Point. Approaching 1 cable off shore clears all dangers including Leade Rocks 3 cables S of the peninsula. Enter the bay avoiding the rock (dr. 1.8m) off the E shore. Anchor in 5m. Exposed to W, S and SE. There is no adequate depth for a yacht in the inner part of the bay where there are moorings for small craft.

Looking across the Sound of Harris towards Leverburgh from Ensay (p. 59)   *Pat and Jill Barron*

The Reef Channel, Berneray from the NE (pp. 56 & 57)   *Alan Nicol*

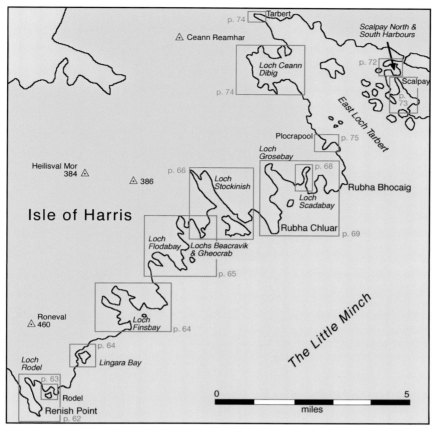

SE Harris key plan

Sound of Harris to East Loch Tarbert

Charts
(ii) 1795 The Little Minch
(iii) 2802 Sound of Harris (Loch Rodel only)
(iii) 2841 Loch Maddy to Loch Resort
OS 18, OS 14

General
A coastline moderately high with steep to shores with undulating harsh, barren slopes echoed on a grander scale by the mountain formations running parallel inland. Comprising some of the oldest geological formations in the world, these desolate slopes set the style for much of Harris and Lewis. They can be astonishingly colourful whether seen edged magnificently against a blue sky or wrapped in wet clinging mist.

Lights
Eilean Glas, Scalpay   Fl(3) W 20s 43m 23M   Wh. Twr. Red bands

Tides
Between Sound of Harris and East Loch Tarbert:
NE-going stream begins —0335 Ullapool (+0430 Dover)
SW-going stream begins +0250 Ullapool (—0130 Dover)
Off the headlands the tidal rate may reach 2 knots in each direction at the spring rate but the streams are very weak in the lochs.

Passage
The coastline from Renish Point at the Sound of Harris to Rubha Bhocaig, at the S entrance to East Loch Tarbert, is a distance of 10 miles and is indented with many lochs which offer anchorage. These include Loch Rodel, Lingara Bay, Loch Finsbay, Lochs Gheocrab and Beacravik, Loch Stockinish and Lochs Grosebay and Scadabay all of which can be used in suitable conditions as shelter or as interesting places to visit.

To clear this coast and remain free of hazards including Nun Rock and Bogha Bhocaig both off Rubha Bhocaig, keep at least 0.5 mile SE of a line from Renish Point to Rubha Bhocaig. In poor visibility the fact that Rubha Chluar is dark and steep to with no offlying islands may be the only distinguishing feature.

Caution
As no large scale recent Admiralty surveys and charts are available a special degree of caution is required when exploring the SE coast of Harris between Renish Point (Sound of Harris) and East Loch Tarbert. It is emphasised that careful pilotage is essential. The plans and text in these sailing directions are indicative only of the hazards which may be met.

Loch Rodel

General The entrance to the loch lies just N of Renish Point. The main part of the loch is exposed to the S and provides temporary anchorage only. Poll an Tighmhail (see opposite) provides better anchorage although entry is only possible when there is sufficient rise of tide.

Tides Const. —0040 Ullapool (—0500 Dover) MHWS 4.6 MHWN 3.5 MTL 2.6 MLWN 1.9 MLWS 0.6

Approach From the Sound of Harris give Renish Point a good offing and beware of vigorous wind against tide conditions which may be present here even in moderate winds. The square tower of St Clement Church on the E side of the loch forms a good landmark. When entering Loch Rodel keep at least 1 cable off the SW side to avoid Duncan Rock (0.3m over it) near the entrance. There is a wreck whose position is uncertain, and a rock near the N'ern corner of the loch.

Anchorage Temporary anchorage whilst waiting for the tide to enter Poll an Tighmhail may be had SW of the shingle beach on the NE side of Loch Rodel. Take care to avoid a drying rock about 100m offshore towards the northern end of the shingle beach. Anchor in 8m, weed. Beware of the dangerous submerged wreck off the point at the head of the loch.

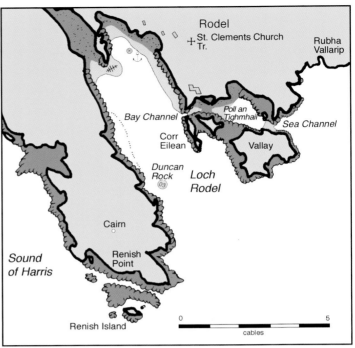

Loch Rodel

The Bay Channel, Rodel at low water springs

Randal Coe

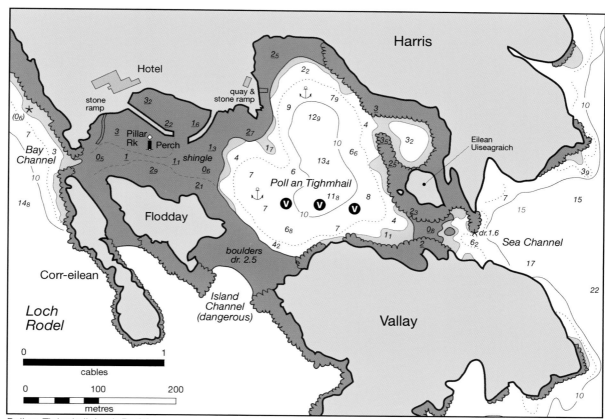

Poll an Tighmhail, Loch Rodel

Rodel (Poll an Tighmhail)

General   A deep pool on the E side Loch Rodel, enclosed by three islets Vallay, Flodday and Corr-eilean which give perfect shelter. Access is governed by the height of the tide as all the channels between the islets dry.

Approach   **Bay Channel** which dries 1.1m is the best entrance. Making entry keep slightly S of mid-channel and steer to pass 15m S of Pillar Rock on which there is a perch, then head towards the N side of the Sea Channel.

When the top of the rectangular Pillar Rock is awash there is 3.1m in the channel. When the base of that rock is awash there is 1.9m in the channel.

Sea Channel entrance (see cover photograph) dries 0.8m with a flat sill covered by heavy kelp. The channel is 20m wide but it must be used with caution if any swell or wave surge is present. Care is required to avoid the rock (dr. 1.6m) at the E end of the channel.

Island Channel dries and due to the rock strewn bottom is dangerous at any state of the tide and should not be used.

Pillar Rock and perch

Anchorage   The centre of the pool is deep with poor holding but **3 visitors moorings** are available on the S side. Anchorage is possible in the N of the pool off the quay and stone ramp in 5m. Swinging is restricted and a kedge may be necessary. It is reported that the restricted space in the NE corner behind a rock (dr. 3.5m) offers anchorage in 3.2m for small vessels. A survey by dinghy or the help of local knowledge is advisable before entering this part of the pool. Anchor bow and stern, taking a line ashore if necessary. Holding ground is reported poor throughout the pool.

Facilities   Recently refurbished Hotel with restaurant. Showers available. Shops, PO and fuel at Leverburgh 2.5 miles.

Interest   St Clement's Church, Rodel is outstanding with very fine carved tombs; one built in 1528 for Alexander MacLeod. The drying harbour was built and channels dredged in the 18th century.

Lingara Bay

Chart   (iii) 2841 Loch Maddy to Loch Resort incl. the Sound of Harris

General   About 2 miles NE of Loch Rodel. Sheltered by Lingarabay Island and islets.

Approach   The E entrance is wide and hazard free but if approaching from the NE note rocks extending 1.5 cables offshore 4 cables E of the entrance.

Anchorage   Anchor just past the S side of Eilean Collam in 5m. The inlet beyond is inaccessible as it is encumbered with rocks. Excellent shelter in winds from the S round by W to N but untenable in E'ly weather.

Facilities   Tel. at Lingarabay.

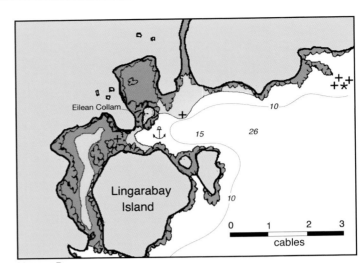

Lingara Bay

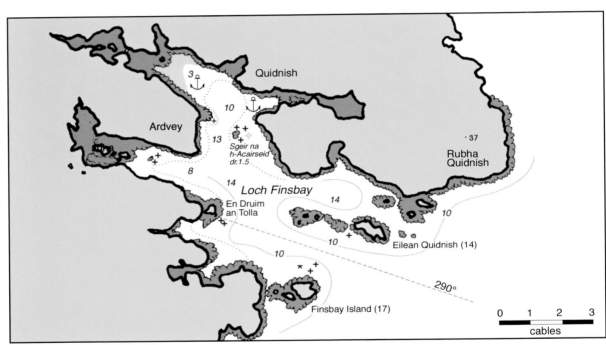

Loch Finsbay

Loch Finsbay

Chart   (ii) 1795 The Little Minch

General   This loch, a mile in length, provides good sheltered anchorage which is relatively easy of access. Finsbay Island is 17m high, green-topped and cliffy. Eilean Quidnish rises to a peak of 14m. Both islands look large and dominate the entrance to the loch.

Tides   Const. —0035 Ullapool (—0455 Dover) MHWS 4.8 MHWN 3.8 ML 2.8 MLWN 2.0 MLWS 0.7

Approach   From the NE keep Rubha Quidnish open of Aird Mhanais to the N until the loch is well open to clear rocks E of Eilean Quidnish. Enter between Finsbay Island and Eilean Quidnish steering for Eilean Druim an Tolla 290°. Hold rather to the Eilean Quidnish side of the channel to avoid reefs 1 cable N of Finsbay Island. Alter course to starboard and keep 0.5 cable off Ardvey to avoid Sgeir na h'Acairseid (dr 1.5m) as well as a reef off Ardvey.

Anchorage   **N of Ardvey,** 4m mud, well sheltered. Smaller yachts may anchor in an arm of the loch 2 cables to the E.

Facilities   Occasional bus.

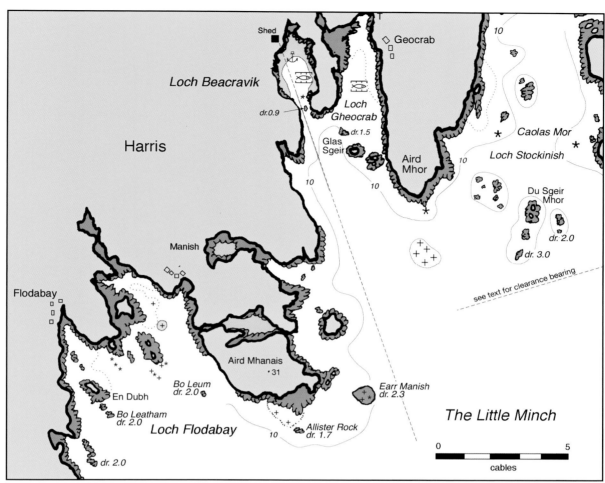

Lochs Flodabay, Beacravik and Gheocrab

Loch Flodabay

General   This loch is encumbered with below water rocks and offers no safe anchorage. It is not recommended. There appears from an old Admiralty Survey to be a clear passage, following the NE shore, to the head of the loch leaving Bogha Leum (dr 2m) to port. Note two further rocks awash near the head of the loch. All three rocks are about 1 cable from the NE shore and should all be left to port.

Caution   Several rocks lie off Aird Mhanais, a low lying headland. These include Allister Rock (dr 1.7m) and Earr Manish (dr 2.3m). Accordingly, when passing Aird Mhanais, give it a wide berth of 5 cables.

Loch Beacravik and Loch Gheocrab

General   About 3 miles from Loch Finsbay, Loch Beacravik offers good shelter.
Loch Gheocrab is not recommended. **The following directions are for Loch Beacravik only.**

Tides   Const. —0035 Ullapool (—0455 Dover) MHWS 4.8 MHWN 3.8 ML 2.8 MLWN 2.0 MLWS 0.7

Approach   **From the SW** note the drying rocks S and E of Aird Mhanais. Keep 5 cables off that point. A large shed at the head of Loch Beacravik is conspic. and when this is in sight it is clear to alter towards the entrance to Loch Beacravik.
From the E note the rocks, one of which has only 0.3m on it 3 cables S of Aird Mhor. **Clearance bearing:** The S end of Shiant Islands in sight S of Rubha Chluar leads S of these and of the rocks in the S entrance to Loch Stockinish. **Caution. If proceeding N to cross the entrance to Loch Stockinish** this clearance bearing must also be used. Beyond Glas Sgeir, at the mouth of Loch Gheocrab, a reef (dr 1.5m) partially blocks the entrance to that loch.

To enter **Loch Beacravik** hold well over to the W side of the narrows to avoid the rocks (dr. 0.9m) which stretch more than half way across the narrows from the E shore and continue to hold to the W shore until the basin opens out.

Anchorage   Anchor in the centre of the basin, off the jetty in 9m. Rocks extend off the burn on the W side and at the head of the basin.

Facilities   Water tap at the large shed. Tel. 0.5 mile S.

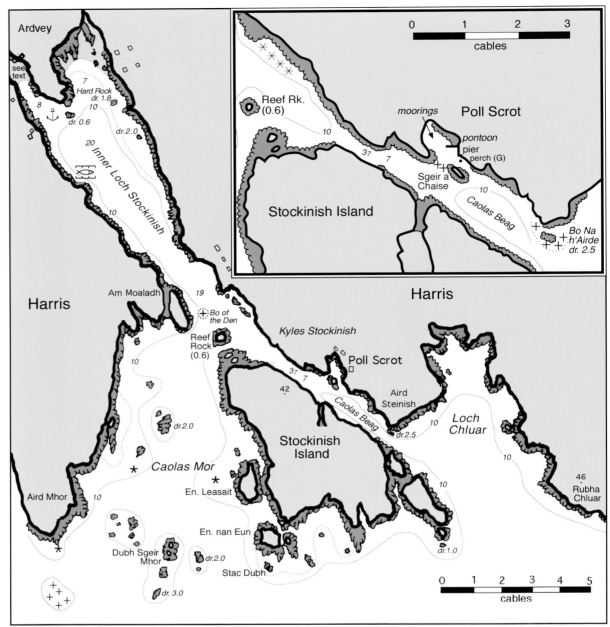

Loch Stockinish with Caolas Beag and Poll Scrot (inset)

Loch Stockinish

General   A loch of stark contrasts between the green sheltered shores at Poll Scrot and Ardvey at the inner end of the loch, and the hard, barren almost snow-like slopes of gneiss on the E shore.

The outer part of Loch Stockinish between Aird Mhor and Stockinish Island, known as Caolas Mor, is rock encumbered and, with only Dubh Sgeir Mhor above water, requires great care in pilotage (see opposite page). It is not recommended as the principal approach channel to the inner loch. At LW or in a heavy sea the rocks in Caolas Mor show or are marked by breakers. NE of Stockinish Island Caolas Beag provides a straightforward passage to the Inner Loch. Loch Chluar which lies immediately to the N of Loch Stockinish cannot be recommended as an anchorage.

Tides   Const. —0027 Ullapool (—0447 Dover) Levels as for Loch Finsbay (p. 64)

Approach   **Caolas Beag** although only 27m wide at its narrowest has a least depth of 3.7m. Bogha na h'Airde (dr 2.5m) lies at the NE side of the entrance to the narrows. Should passage be made before half tide Bogha na h'Airde will show. In any event keep to the Stockinish side at the entrance to the narrows. If making for Poll Scrot pass E of the islet in the narrows and leave the perch opposite the N end of the islet to starboard before altering towards the pontoon jetty.

Anchorage   **Poll Scrot.** NW of Sgeir a Chaise in Caolas Beag in 4m. Very limited swinging room but there is a substantial pontoon with a depth of 3m alongside. **Facilities** Water by hose. Diesel (key card needed, see p.5).

Caolas Beag, looking NW to Loch Stockinish   *David Martin*

Inner Loch Stockinish

Approach On emerging from the narrows keep the channel open astern for 4 cables to clear Bo of the Den, a rock with 1.8m over it which lies 0.5 cable E of Am Moaladh, a prominent tidal island on the W side of the entrance to the inner loch. The inner loch is clear up to its head where Hard Rock (dr 1.8m) lies 1 cable E of the point which divides the loch. Note particularly the rock drying 0.6m extending 1 cable SE from this point.

Anchorage At the entrance to the NW arm of the loch, 9m sand. Smaller yachts or those with limited draft will find anchorage within the arm. **Caution.** A cable reaches across midway up the NW arm of Loch Stockinish at a height of 6m above sea level.

Facilities Shop and PO at Kyles Stockinish near Poll Scrot.

Alternative approach **The approach by Caolas Mor** to the Inner Loch demands great care. From the S aim to pass between Dubh Sgeir Mhor, which always shows, and Eilean nan Eun. The passage to the inner loch is best made within 2.5 hours of LW when the reefs which dry 2m will show. The main dangers are an extensive reef (dr 2m) 1 cable E of Dubh Sgeir Mhor, a rock awash W of Eilean Leasaid, and an extensive reef (dr 2m) 4 cables N of Dubh Sgeir Mhor. To avoid these pass 1 cable W of Eilean nan Eun and associated islets then 1.5 cables W of Eilean Leasaid. With Eilean Leasaid abeam head midway between Am Moaladh and Reef Rock, leaving the reef (dr 2m) to port. After reaching Reef Rock make for the NE shore in order to avoid Bo of the Den with 1.8m over it. Hold this course until Caolas Beag begins to open up when a turn may be made to port to enter the inner loch.

Poll Scrot catch   *Arthur Houston*

Loch Scadabay

Arthur Houston

Loch Grosebay

Charles Tait

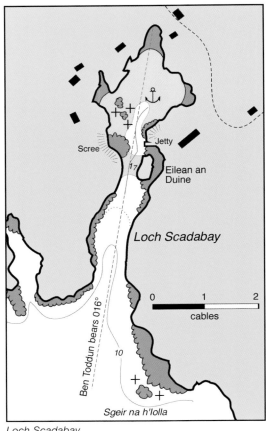

Loch Scadabay

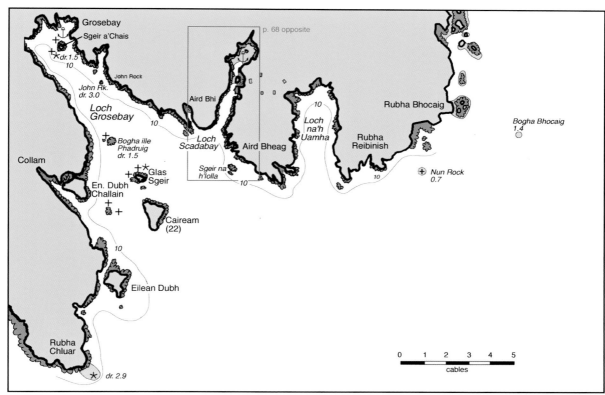

Loch Grosebay

Loch Grosebay

General   Loch Grosebay offers only moderately good shelter at its head and is exposed to E'ly winds.

Approach   If coming from the N keep 0.5 mile off the Reibinish Peninsula to avoid Bogha Bhocaig with 1.4m over it and Nun Rock with 0.7m over it which lie 4 cables E and S respectively of Rubha Bhocaig. On entry, keep 2 cables off the NE shore of Loch Grosebay to clear Sgeir na h'Iolla at the S side of the entrance to Loch Scadabay. Note that whatever the direction of approach, the islands, islets and reefs off the SW shore of the loch, Eilean Dubh, Cairearn, Glas Sgeir and Bogha ille Phadruig (dr 1.5m) should all be left to port. Nearing the head of the loch, tend to the W shore to clear John Rock (dr 3m) and Sgeir a'Chais with its rock (dr 1.5m) which extends SW 0.5 cable.

Anchorage   N of Sgeir a'Chais in 9m. Not well sheltered.

Facilities   Garage and workshop for repairs at Grosebay village. (K. Maclennan, tel. 01859 511253). Small slipway.

Loch Scadabay

General   Loch Scadabay offers very good protection and, although the entrance is narrow, is not difficult to negotiate. It is a little over 2 miles from Poll Scrot, Loch Stockinish to Loch Scadabay.

Tides   Const. —0027 Ullapool (—0447 Dover) MHWS 4.8 MHWN 3.8 ML 2.8 MLWN 2.0 MLWS 0.7

Approach   **From the East and North** keep at least 5 cables off Rubha Bhocaig and the coast S of that headland to avoid Bogha Bhocaig with 1.4m over it, and Nun rock with 0.6m over it. On altering W'wards to acquire the narrow entrance to Loch Scadabay do not be deceived by the first wide inlet, Loch na h'Uamha. Continue keeping 2 cables off shore to avoid Sgeir na h'Iolla. **The narrow entrance will open up when Toddun (526m) N of East Loch Tarbert bears 016°.**

     From the South keep 3 cables off Rubha Chluar and Eilean Dubh and then alter towards the entrance. If Toddun is not visible then the SE side of Caiream in line astern with Rubha Chluar leads to the W side of the outer entrance clear of rocks. **Within the entrance** keep mid-channel and pass W of Eilean an Duine through a narrow cleft 30m wide with steep sides and a least a depth of 1.7m over a sandy bottom. Bear to starboard towards the stone jetty to avoid drying rocks off scree at the foot of the cliff on the port hand and follow the rocky point round to starboard to avoid drying rocks to port which lie on the W side of the pool.

Anchorage   In the centre of the pool clear of rocks on the W side in 1.8m. Very soft mud. Yachts of deep draft sink in without listing. Note: Loch na h'Uamh is unsuitable for anchorage but an Admiralty survey shows no hidden dangers.

Facilities   Small shop. Tel. Water at houses. Centre for Harris Tweed.

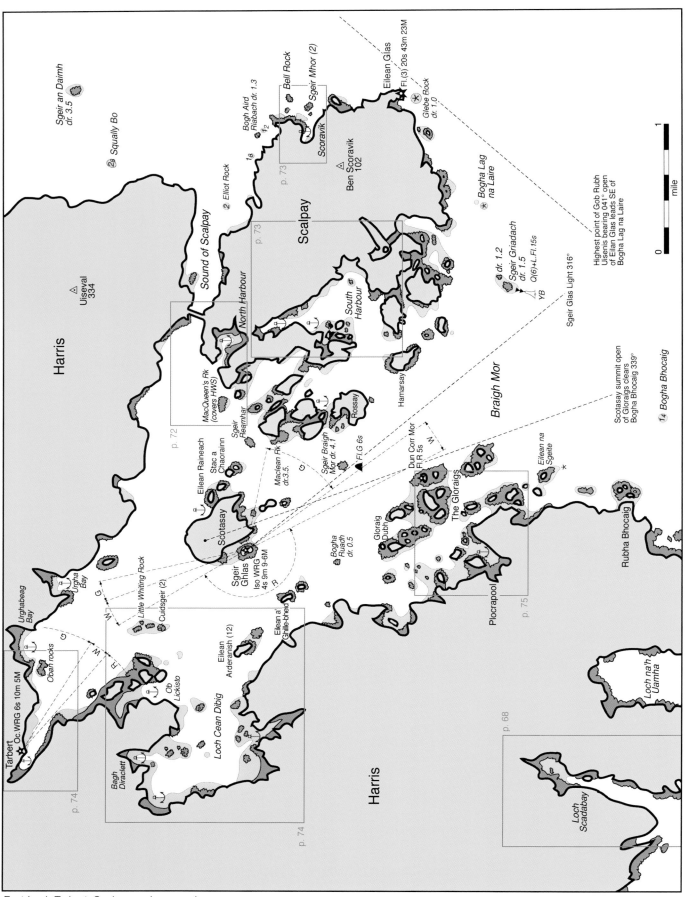

East Loch Tarbert, Scalpay and approaches

East Loch Tarbert, Harris

Charts

(ii) 1794 North Minch - Southern part
(ii) 1795 The Little Minch
(iii) 2905 East Loch Tarbert
OS 14

General

East Loch Tarbert provides many well-sheltered anchorages particularly at Scalpay, the island on the N side of the entrance, and Tarbert at the head of the loch. It is an excellent place of arrival at the Outer Hebrides from the N of Skye, combining a shorter crossing of the Little Minch with relative ease of access. The loch has many rocks and must be navigated with care. The detailed Chart 2905 is essential when navigating outside the principal approach channels of Braigh Mor and the Sound of Scalpay.

It is 25 miles from Lochmaddy, North Uist to Tarbert, Harris and about 30 miles from Tarbert, Harris to Stornoway, Isle of Lewis.

Scalpay, the largest island in the loch, is well populated. Scotasay, an island with a distinctive shape, lies near the centre within the loch, 1 mile NW of Scalpay. The passage between Scalpay and Scotasay should be navigated with great care to avoid a number of drying reefs including Sgeir Braigh Mor, Maclean Rock, Sgeir Reamhar and MacQueen's Rock which covers at HWS. The Gloraigs and many other islets give the S half of the loch a complex appearance. This area has innumerable islands, islets, reefs and rocks and can only be safely navigated with Chart 2905.

Tides

Const. —0027 Ullapool (—0447 Dover) MHWS 5.0 MHWN 3.7 ML 2.9 MLWN 2.1 MLWS 0.8
Streams in Braigh Mor and the Sound of Scalpay
NW-going stream begins —0520 Ullapool (+0145 Dover)
SE-going stream begins +0105 Ullapool (—0325 Dover)
The NW-going flood stream in the Little Minch runs into East Loch Tarbert through Braigh Mor, then N between Scalpay and Scotasay, and E out of the loch through the Sound of Scalpay.
The spring rate in each direction in the Sound of Scalpay is from 1.5 to 2 knots but less elsewhere. The streams in the inner part of the loch beyond Scotasay are imperceptible.

Lights

Eilean Glas Lt Ho.	Fl (3) W 20s 43m 23M	Racon (T) White tower, red bands
Braigh Mor Entrance Channel		
Sgeir Griadach	Q (6) + LFl 15s	S Cardinal light buoy
Sgeir Braigh Mor	Fl. G 6s	Green con light buoy on the N side of the channel
Dunn Corr Mor	Fl. R 5s 10m 5M	Wh painted structure on the S side of the channel
Sgeir Ghlas	Iso WRG 4s 9m 9—6M	Wh Round conc. twr. Sectors as plan
Tarbert Ferry Pier	2FG (vert) 10m 5M	Grey column
	Oc WRG 6s 10m 5M	(Occasional when ferry expected) Centre of W sector 302°
Ro- Ro terminal	2FG (vert) 7m 5M	Grey column on dolphin

Approach

Braigh Mor, the entrance channel to East Loch Tarbert S of Scalpay has two dangerous rocks on the N side of the entrance, Bogha Lag na Laire (just dries) and Sgeir Griadach (dr. 1.5m) marked by a S Cardinal light buoy Q (6) + LFl 15s. Beware also of Bogha Ruadh (dr. 0.5m) which is unmarked on the SW side of Braigh Mor 4 cables NNW of Gloraig Dubh, the most N'ly of the Gloraigs. Sgeir Braigh Mor (dr. 4.1) on the NE side of the channel is marked by a green conical buoy Fl G 6s. The SW extremity of Eilean Arderanish bearing 303° and open NE of Eilean a'Ghille-bheid, 4 cables SE of Eilean Arderanish, leads about 1 cable NE of Bogha Ruadh.

From the S keep 0.5 mile off Rubha Bhocaig to avoid Bogha Bhocaig (1.4m over it). The summit of Scotasay bearing 339° and open of the Gloraigs leads SE of this rock. **Or,** to pass between Bogha Bhocaig and the hazards E of Rubha Bhocaig keep the E extremity of Eilean na Sgaite, 6 cables N of Rubha Bhocaig, in line with the W extremity of Dun Corr Mor with its white painted light structure bearing 353°. Head N leaving the Gloraigs to port. Identify the entrance to the South Harbour, Scalpay between Rossay and Hamarsay, or, if making for Tarbert, identify the channel between Dun Corr Mor and the Green con. light buoy (Fl G 6s) at Sgeir Braigh Mor. Proceed to Tarbert at the head of the loch as described on p. 74. If making for Scalpay Harbour see under Scalpay (p. 72).

From the N or E head SW from a position 0.5 mile E of the Eilean Glas Lighthouse to avoid Bogha Lag na Laire (just dries) and Sgeir Griadach (dr 1.5m) marked by a S Cardinal light buoy Q (6) + LFl 15s, both dangerous rocks 4 and 5 cables respectively S of Scalpay. Maintain a SW'ly course until Sgeir Ghlas with its small white light tower SW of Scotasay is in line, bearing 316°, with Sgeir Braigh Mor, marked by a Green con. buoy (Fl G 6s).

Note: The highest point of Gob Rubh'Uisenis (not the extremity) Lat. 57° 56.2' N, 6° 28.5'W bearing 041° open of Eilean Glas Lighthouse leads SE of Bogha Lag na Laire. The highest part of Scotasay bearing 319° open of the SW tip of Rossay leads SW of Sgeir Griadach. By night the white sector of Sgeir Ghlas light on the SW side of Scotasay leads clear of all dangers.

Scalpay

Charts
(ii) 1795 The Little Minch
(iii) 2905 East Loch Tarbert
OS 14

General
Scalpay Sound provides a straightforward approach to Scalpay North Harbour and Tarbert at the head of East Loch Tarbert. Scalpay Bridge has **20m clearance** and lights on N side Iso G 4s; at centre Occ W 6s; S side Iso R 4s.

Approach
When approaching Scalpay Sound **from the S or E** give the E and NE side of Scalpay a fair berth to avoid reefs and rocks extending offshore more than a cable. Open the Sound well up before heading W to avoid Elliot Rock. **From the N** keep 0.7 mile offshore to avoid Sgeir an Daimh (dr. 3.5m) about 1 mile NE of Rubha Crago (see plan p. 70). Enter the Sound following the N shore to avoid Elliot Rock.

After entering the Sound note that rocks extend from the N shore at the old ferry slip. Pass under the bridge (clearance 20m). Once through the Sound there is easy access to North Harbour, Scalpay, or to Tarbert at the head of the loch by proceeding in mid channel leaving Cuidsgeir (2) and Little Whiting Rock (dr 3.0m) to port and passing S of the Oban Rocks.

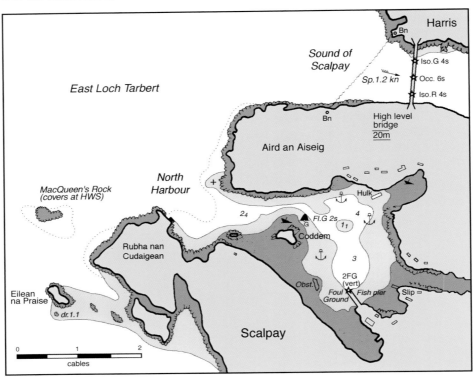

Scalpay North Harbour

Scalpay, North Harbour

Lights
At entrance Green Con light buoy FL G 2s
At pier 2FG (vert)

Approach
From the Sound of Scalpay note MacQueen's Rock, SW of the harbour entrance which covers at HWS. Aird an Aiseig on the port hand should be given a berth of 0.5 cable and a course a little N of mid-channel taken N of the Green con. buoy inside the entrance. Turn to starboard and head for the pier before reaching the 1.1m submerged rocky patch 0.5 cable E of the Green con. buoy N of Coddem Island.

From the Braigh Mor channel. After passing E or W of Sgeir Braigh Mor make for Stac a Chaorainn lying 2 cables E of the E extremity of Scotasay. Sgeir Reamhar (covers at HWS) is best left to starboard and, similarly, pass 1 cable W of McQueen's Rock (covers at HWS) lying W of the entrance to the North Harbour.
Alternatively pass W and N of Scotasay before altering towards Scalpay North Harbour entrance.

Anchorage
The pier has 2m on both sides. Tie up alongside the fishing vessels at weekends. At other times seek permission or anchor, taking precautions due to the chance of having a foul anchor. In N'ly winds better shelter is obtained anchoring S of the hulk in the NE corner of the harbour or 1 cable W clear of moorings. Shallow draft vessels may tie alongside the hulk on its inner (N'ly) side. In W to NW fresh to strong winds good holding is reported in the lee of Coddem but beware of obstruction area indicated on the plan above.

Facilities
Shops, tel., PO, crafts. Calor gas. Water at pier. Diesel (key card needed, see p.5). Mobile bank on Tuesdays.

Scalpay, South Harbour

Approach From Braigh Mor enter between Hamarsay and Rossay, keep mid-channel until clear of the rock (dr 1.7m) SE of Raarem, an islet to port. Scalpay House, which has two broad chimneys, on rising ground at the head of the harbour bearing 338° and just open E of the SW shore, leads E of the rocks SE of Raarem. Turn towards the inner harbour, keeping well towards the NW side to avoid Boundary Rock with less than 0.4m over it.

Anchorage Anchor 1.5 cables S of the entrance to the inner harbour in 13m medium black mud. Or, to obtain better shelter, enter the inner harbour holding close to the NW side to avoid extensive drying rocks on the E side. Anchor in 4m in the centre of the pool clear of local boats which restrict swinging room. Holding reported poor.

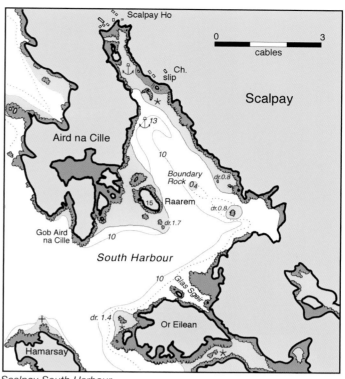

Scalpay South Harbour

Scalpay North Harbour

Arthur Houston

Scoravick

Anchorage This bay on the E side of Scalpay, a little over 0.5 mile N of Eilean Glas Lighthouse, is a useful stopping over place during passage making and avoids the extra distance to North Harbour, Scalpay. Enter mid-channel, leaving Sgeir Mhor (2) lying in the centre of the approach to the bay and a rock (dr 2.1m) on the starboard hand. Anchor on the S side in good holding ground in 5m. Well protected from N to W and SW. Exposed to S and E'ly winds.

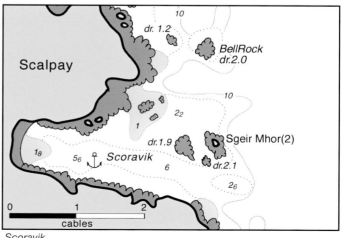

Scoravik

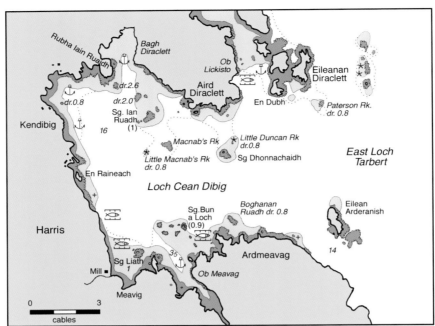

Loch Ceann Dibig

Loch Ceann Dibig

Chart   (iii) 2905 East Loch Tarbert

Anchorage   **Ob Lickisto** at the N entrance of Loch Ceann Dibig, on the W side of Eileanan Diraclett. Note Paterson Rock (dr. 0.8m) 1 cable SE of Eileanan Diraclett. Rubha Crago, at the entrance to the Sound of Scalpay, shut in behind Scotasay, leads S of this rock. As soon as the entrance W of Eilean Dubh is open, alter course N'wards. Anchor off the W shore of Eilean na h'Airigne, N of Eilean Dubh. Drying rocks restrict anchoring further in. Good holding.

Bagh Diraclett on the N side of Loch Ceann Dibig. Pass S of Sgeir Dhonnachaidh (Duncan Rock) which should be kept open of the N end of Scotasay until the W side of Bagh Diraclett bears due N. Head N to within a cable of Rubha Iain Ruaidh leaving Little Macnab's Rock (dr 0.8m) and Sgeir Ian Ruadh (1m) to starboard. Note that the rocks (dr 2.6m and 2.0m) on either hand at the entrance should be visible within 2 hours of LW. It may be difficult to enter safely until these drying rocks are visible. Anchorage is also available on either side of the rock (dr 0.8m) off **Kendibig**. Good holding.

Ob Meavag on the S side of Loch Ceann Dibig. In the approach keep Sgeir Ghlas light open of Eilean Arderanish to clear rocks on the S side of the loch. Do not turn to port until Meavag Mill bears 200° to avoid drying rocks 1 cable W of Sgeir Bun a'Loch (0.9m). Steer on this bearing until Sgeir Bun a'Loch is open N of Eilean Arderanish then turn to enter the bay. Anchor within the entrance in 3m mud. Well sheltered with good holding. A kedge may be necessary in cross winds to prevent swinging. Exposed to NW winds.

Tarbert

Approach   When making for Tarbert pass between Dun Corr Mor and the Green con. light buoy S of Sgeir Braigh Mor and steer for Sgeir Ghlas, SW of Scotasay. Pass W of Sgeir Ghlas and head in a N'ly direction towards the W side of Urgha Bay. Maintain this N'ly course until clear of Cuidsgeir (2) and Little Whiting Rock (dr 3.0m) to port and then turn to port and head for Tarbert keeping mid-channel until well clear of the Oban Rocks to starboard and Sgeir Bhuidhe to port.

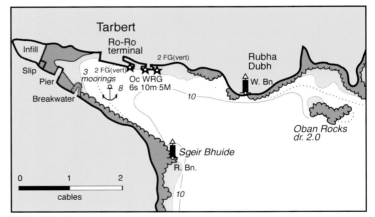

Tarbert Harbour

Anchorage   Tarbert Anchor SW of the Ro-Ro pier as far inshore as depth and moorings permit and clear of the ferry's approach to the pier.

Facilities   Hotels, shops, PO, tel., bank, craft shops. Harris Tweed shop. Petrol and diesel at nearby garage. Calor gas. Water from tap at pier. Tourist information centre. Car hire and taxi service. Car ferry to Lochmaddy, North Uist and Uig, Skye.

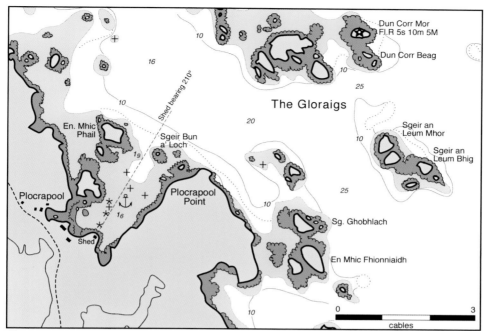

Plocrapool and The Gloraigs

Plocrapool

Approach This anchorage lies inshore of the Gloraigs. Approach from W of the Gloraigs or S of Dun Corr Mor which is shaped a bit like a sugar loaf. Pass W of the above-water rock, Sgeir Bun a' Loch, in the middle of the entrance to Plocrapool Bay, with a somewhat inconspic. dilapidated corrugated iron shed just above the SW shore bearing 210°, Although the chart indicates rocks less than 2m in the outer part of the bay these are likely to be hazardous only at LW. Hold to the E side of the bay clear of drying rocks and anchor as far in as depth will allow.

Anchorages on the North Side of East Loch Tarbert

Anchorage **Urgha Bay** on the N shore about 1 mile E of Tarbert. Good holding. Protected from N winds (see plan p. 70).

Urghabeag Bay a little over 0.5 mile E of Tarbert. Note the Oban Rocks and large reef at the W side of the entrance. Anchor near the head of the bay in 2.5m but clear of the drying reefs extending 0.5c on the W side of the bay.

Scotasay on the NE side of the island in the NW part of the bay W of Eilean Raineach in 3m. A drying rock lies 3c. offshore NW of Eilean Raineach. Well sheltered from S, SW or W winds.

Tarbert Harbour

Arthur Houston

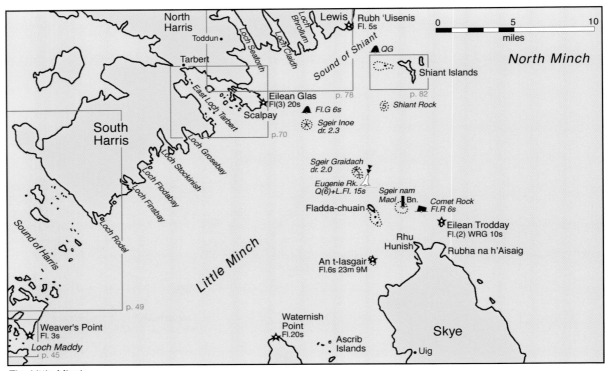

The Little Minch

Crossing the Little Minch

Chart   (ii) 1795 The Little Minch
            (ii) 1794 North Minch (Southern Part)
            (ii) 2210 (for North Skye)

General   The Little Minch between Skye and Harris is a dangerous area of sea in bad weather conditions. The effect of wind, tidal streams and, in places, the nature of the sea bottom results in steep waves. Passage planning should allow for tidal flow in the Minches.

Distances   North Skye to Tarbert Harris 20 miles
                North Skye to Lochmaddy 29 miles.
                Loch Dunvegan to Tarbert, Harris 29 miles.
                Dunvegan to Lochmaddy 21 miles.
                North Skye to Stornoway, Isle of Lewis 30 miles

Tides   **In the channel between Rubha na h'Aiseig (N. Skye) and Eilean Troddday**, the streams run E and W. following the Skye coastline.
            E-going stream begins —0415 Ullapool (+0400 Dover)
            W-going stream begins +0210 Ullapool (—0210 Dover)
            The spring rate in each direction is 2.5 knots. There are eddies in the bay between Rubha na h'Aiseig and Eilean Troddday.

            Between Eilean Glas and Sgeir Inoe (dr 1.8m) the streams usually run ENE and SW although at times the streams are much affected by wind especially at neaps.

            At springs ENE-going stream begins —0315 Ullapool (+0500 Dover)
                           SW-going stream begins +0310 Ullapool (—0100 Dover)
                           The ENE-going stream has a spring rate of 2.5 knots. The SW-going stream is somewhat weaker.

            At neaps NNE-going stream starting at —0505 Ullapool (+0300 Dover) turns gradually to the E and runs for 8.5 hrs.
                         SW-going stream begins +0320 Ullapool (—0100 Dover) and runs for 4 hrs.

            Between Rubh 'Uisenis and the Shiant Islands in the Sound of Shiant
            NE-going stream begins —0315 Ullapool (+0500 Dover)
            SW-going stream begins +0310 Ullapool (—0100 Dover)
            The spring rate in each direction is 3 to 4 knots.

            The streams around the Shiants are much affected by the wind especially at neaps. The Shiant Islands lie across the direction of the stream, and eddies occur near the islands. For details see p. 82.

Caution   There are heavy overfalls in the Sound of Shiant mid-channel area approximately 2 miles W of the Shiants Green con. light buoy (Qk.G) and about 2 miles SE of the entrance to Loch Bhrollum. **This area is particularly dangerous when strong NE winds interact with the NE-going tidal stream.**

Crossing the Little Minch (continued)

Lights			
	Eilean Trodday	Fl (2) WRG 10s 52m 12-9 M	Wh framework Twr
	Waternish Point	Fl. 20s 21m 8M	Wh framework Twr
	Eilean Glas Lt Ho	Fl (3) 20s 43m 23M	Wh Twr Red bands
	An t-Iasgair Bn.	Fl. 6s 23m 9M	Metal pole
	Comet Rock Lt buoy	Fl.R 6s	R can buoy
	Eugenie Rock Lt Buoy	Q(6) + L.Fl. 15s	S cardinal buoy
	Sgeir Inoe Lt buoy	Fl.G 6s	G conical buoy, Racon (M)
	Shiants Lt buoy	Qk.G	G conical buoy
	Rubh' Uisenis	Fl 5s 24m 11M	Wh Twr

Directions

From North Skye to Tarbert, Harris. The best course is to pass 1 mile N of both Eilean Trodday and Comet Rock which is marked by a Red can light buoy (Fl R 6s). Maintain course to pass well N of Sgeir nam Maol marked by a green beacon, 12 metres in height. The aim is to avoid overfalls, also the Eugenie Rock (dr 2m) and Sgeir Graidach lying 3 cables NW of that rock. In good visibility a course towards Toddun, a conspic. conical hill on Harris, clears these hazards. Leave the Green con light buoy (Fl G 6s bell) marking Sgeir Inoe (dr 2.3m) to port. Once clear of this drying rock alter course for the Sound of Scalpay, N of Scalpay, to enter East Loch Tarbert provided your masthead height is less than 20m, being the height at the bridge!

If making for the entrance channel Braigh Mor S of Scalpay, beware of Sgeir Inoe (dr 1.8m) which lies 3 miles ESE of the Eilean Glas Light Tower. A Green con light buoy is positioned 8 cables N of Sgeir Inoe. Eilean Glas Light Tower in line with the summit of Tirga Mor (58° 00'N, 6° 59'W), the first hill N of Tarbert, bearing 308° leads 4 cables SW of Sgeir Inoe.

From North Skye to Loch Maddy. Pass between Eilean Trodday and Skye when tidal and sea conditions are suitable. Thereafter the passage to Loch Maddy is straightforward.

From Uig (Loch Snizort, Skye) to Tarbert, Harris. Set a course for the light tower on Eilean Glas, Scalpay for subsequent entry by the Sound of Scalpay but taking into account any tidal set towards Sgeir Inoe, and the height restriction of 20m at the bridge over the Sound. Alternatively enter East Loch Tarbert through Braigh Mor, S of Scalpay. This S entrance requires greater navigational care (see p. 71) but there is not the masthead height restriction of 20m at the bridge over Scalpay Sound.

From Loch Dunvegan to Tarbert, Harris. Once clear of Loch Dunvegan, head for Eilean Glas light tower, Scalpay. Then enter East Loch Tarbert as for the passage from Uig (see above).

East Loch Tarbert to Stornoway

Charts

(ii) 1794 North Minch (Southern Part)
(iii) 2529 Approaches to Stornoway, Stornoway Harbour, Loch Erisort
OS 14, OS 8

Passage

It is about 27 miles from North Harbour, Scalpay, Harris to Stornoway.
If proceeding NE'wards to cross the entrances to Loch Trollamarig, Loch Seaforth and Loch Claidh keep SE of a line from Rubha Crago, the NE side of the Sound of Scalpay, to Rubh 'a Bhaird on the W side of the entrance to Loch Bhrollum. Keeping SE of this line and then a few cables offshore and clear of the entrances to all lochs further N, provides safe passage to Stornoway.

The lochs on the SE of the Isle of Lewis comprising Loch Seaforth, Loch Claidh, Loch Valamus (Bhalamuis) and Loch Bhrollum, all reach N'wards into a particularly mountainous and isolated part of the Isle of Lewis. They are all exposed to S'ly winds and subject to heavy squalls. Protection may be limited. Northwards from Gob Rubh'Uisenis the coast is less dramatic and secure anchorage is to be found principally in Loch Shell, Loch Mariveg (Mharabhig), Loch Erisort and Loch Grimshader.

Lights			
	Eilean Glas Lt Ho	Fl (3) 20s 43m 23M	Wh Twr Red bands
	Sgeir Inoe Lt buoy	Fl.G 6s	G conical buoy, Racon (M)
	Shiants Lt buoy	Qk.G	G conical buoy
	Rubh' Uisenis	Fl 5s 24m 11M	Wh Twr
	Arnish Point	Fl.WR.10s 17m 9/7M	Wh Round Twr (W sector 102°—109° (7°))

Tides

For tidal streams between **Eilean Glas and Sgeir Inoe** and between **Rubh' Uisenish and the Shiant Islands in the Sound of Shiant** see p. 76 opposite.

Between Gob na Milaid and Kebock Head and off these headlands the tide reaches 3 knots at springs.
N-going stream begins —0305 Ullapool (+0500 Dover)
S-going stream begins +0220 Ullapool (—0200 Dover)
The tides N of Kebock Head and as far as Tiumpan Head on the Eye Peninsular are weak.

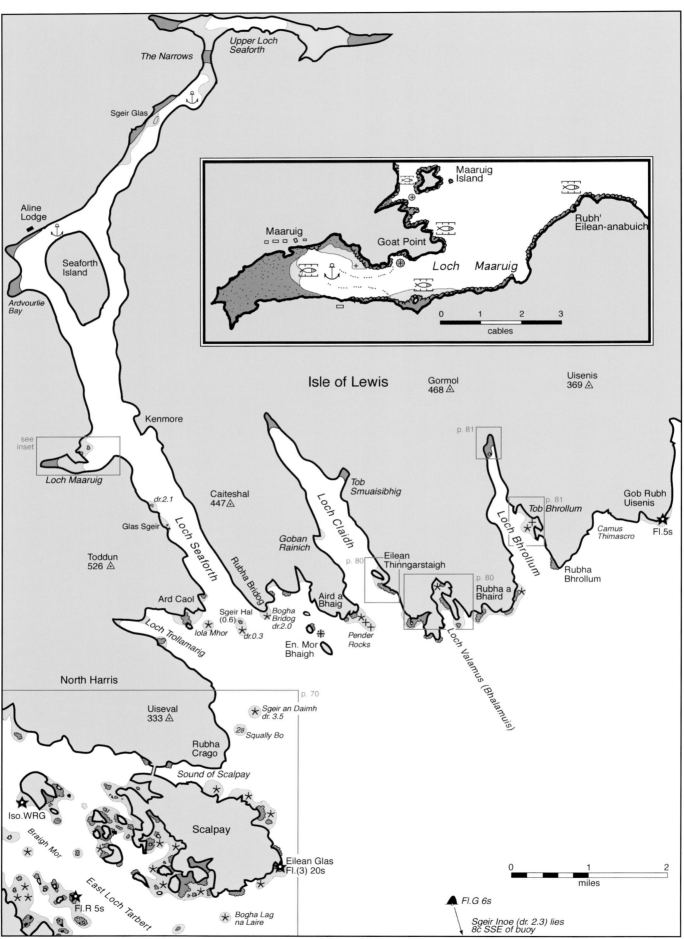

The Narrows

Upper Loch
Seaforth

Sgeir Glas

Aline
Lodge

Seaforth
Island

Ardvourlie
Bay

Inset (Loch Maaruig):

Maaruig
Island

Maaruig

Goat Point

Loch Maaruig

Rubh'
Eilean-anabuich

0   1   2   3
cables

Isle of Lewis

Gormol
468 △

Uisenis
369 △

Kenmore

see
inset

Loch Maaruig

p. 81

p. 81

Tob Bhrollum

Gob Rubh
Uisenis

dr.2.1

Caiteshal
447 △

Tob
Smuaisibhig

Loch Claidh

Camus
Thimascro

Fl.5s

Glas Sgeir

Loch Seaforth

Rubha Bridog

Goban
Rainich

p. 80

Eilean
Thinngarstaigh

Loch Bhrollum

Toddun
526 △

Ard Caol

Sgeir Hal
(0.6)

Iola Mhor

dr.0.3

Bogha
Bridog
dr.2.0

Aird a
Bhaig

p. 80

Rubha a
Bhaird

Rubha
Bhrollum

Loch Trollamarig

En. Mor
Bhaigh

Pender
Rocks

Loch Valamus (Bhalamuis)

North Harris

p. 70

Uiseval
333 △

Sgeir an Daimh
dr. 3.5

28   Squally Bo

Rubha
Crago

Sound of Scalpay

Scalpay

Iso.WRG

Braigh Mor

Eilean Glas
Fl.(3) 20s

Fl.R 5s

East Loch Tarbert

Bogha Lag
na Laire

Fl.G 6s

Sgeir Inoe (dr. 2.3) lies
8c SSE of buoy

0   1   2
miles

Loch Seaforth with (inset) Loch Maaruig and other lochs on the SE coast of Harris

Loch Seaforth

Chart

(ii) 1794 North Minch (Southern Part)
OS 14

General

Loch Seaforth reaches about 9 miles N'wards into a mountainous region of Harris and Lewis. As a result of the wind accelerating down the steep mountainous slopes on either side of the loch and because of the narrowness of the loch, the squalls are extremely sudden and violent from unpredictable directions.

About 6 miles from the entrance lies Seaforth Island with a clear passage on either side. Beyond the island the loch continues NE'wards to the Narrows which lead to Upper Loch Seaforth. It is inadvisable for any yacht to navigate through the Narrows where it is reported the streams run at 7 knots springs.

In the outer approaches to Loch Seaforth, that is in the the area between Rubha Crago at the NE side of the Sound of Scalpay and Aird a'Bhaigh at the W side of the entrance to Loch Claidh, there are a number of islets and rocks most of which can be seen. In particular **Sgeir an Daimh** lying about 9 cables NNE of Rubha Crago, although charted as 'dr. 3.5m', is reported never to cover and to be visible in all conditions except in a flat calm near HW. **For the hazards at the entrance to Loch Seaforth see the 'Approach' paragraph below.**

On the E side of the entrance to Loch Seaforth a series of above and below water rocks extends 4 cables S'wards from Aird a'Bhaigh (the W point of Loch Claidh) terminating in Pender rock (with 0.3m over it). Between Aird a'Bhaigh and Rubha Bridog, the entrance point to Loch Seaforth, are three islets - Eilean Mor a'Bhaigh, Dubh a'Bhaigh and Beag a'Bhaigh.

Sgeir Hal, the key to navigating the entrance to the loch, lies 4 cables SW of Rubha Bridog. It is believed to be about 0.6m high, although charted at 2.0m high, and may be difficult to spot at HW. Bogha Ruadh, lying 1 cable S of Sgeir Hal, dries 0.3m. Bogha Bridog (dr 2.0m) lies 1 cable SSE off Rubha Bridog.

Loch Trollamarig, to the W of the entrance to Loch Seaforth, is not a safe anchorage.

Tides

Const. —0027 Ullapool (—0447 Dover)
MHWS 5.0   MHWN 3.7   ML 2.9   MLWN 2.1   MLWS 0.8
Streams in the entrance and within Loch Seaforth do not exceed 1 knot until the Narrows leading to Upper Loch Seaforth.
In-going stream begins +0610 Ullapool (+0150 Dover)
Out-going stream begins —0015 Ullapool (—0435 Dover)

Approach

From the S, when passing Eilean Glas Light tower on Scalpay, the remarkable conical mountain Toddun, indicates the SW entrance to the loch. Pass 0.5 mile E of Eilean Glas light tower and then steer towards Sgeir Hal, the small islet in the entrance to the loch (see above), passing more than 2 cables E of Sgeir an Daimh, which, as mentioned above, has been reported never to cover.

When approaching the entrance from the S aim to pass either W of Sgeir Hal avoiding Bogha Ruadh (dr 0.3m) lying 1 cable S of Sgeir Hal, and Iola Mhor lying 2.5c S of Ard Caol the W point of the entrance; or E of Sgeir Hal holding close to the NE shore. This latter course is recommended but be aware of Bogha Ruadh, and Bogha Bridog (dr. 2.0m) lying a cable SSE of Rubha Bridog, the E point of the entrance. See clearance bearing below.

From the E pass S of Eilean Mor a'Bhaigh and then alter towards Rubha Bridog and hold close to the NE shore leaving Sgeir Hal to port. Caution. Take care to avoid Bogha Bhridog which lies 1 cable SSE of Rubha Bhridog. **Clearance bearing:** The S point of Loch Maaruig, an inlet on the W side of the loch, open of Rubha Bridog leads close W of Bogha Bridog.

Within the loch the W shore is free from dangers from Ard Caol to Seaforth Island except for a rock 75m offshore which dries 2.1m. This rock lies 3 cables N of Glas Sgeir, an islet 1 mile S of the entrance to Loch Maaruig. The E side of the loch is clear.

Anchorage

Loch Maaruig on the W side of the loch 2.5 miles from the entrance. The awash rock SW of Goat point is cleared by keeping Goat Point open of the S point of the entrance. Anchor off Maaruig W of Goat point in 7m, mud. Well sheltered but large fish farms are moored here (see plan opposite).

Aline Lodge. Anchor N of Seaforth Island in 7m, 0.5 mile E of Aline Lodge which is visible from the entrance to the loch (see photograph p. 84).

S of the Narrows in the SE corner 0.5 mile from the Narrows. Approaching from Seaforth Island this NE arm has several dangerous rocks off the NW shore. Leave the islet Sgeir Glas to port.

Eilean Thinngarstaigh anchorage, Loch Claidh (p.80)   *Jane Routh*

Loch Claidh

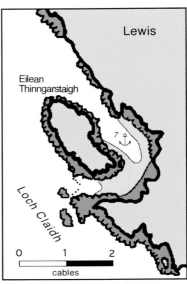

Eilean Thinngarstaigh anchorage

Chart (ii) 1794 North Minch (Southern Part)
OS 14

Tides Const. —0027 Ullapool (—0447 Dover)
MHWS 5.0 MHWN 3.7 ML 2.9 MLWN 2.1 MLWS 0.8

General About 2 miles E from Loch Seaforth and 2 miles W of Loch Bhrollum. Loch Claidh has hills of moderate height at its entrance but becomes mountainous at the head of the loch. It can appear desolate, grim and forbidding in appearance. Loch Claidh is easier to identify and enter than Loch Bhrollum, and is 3 miles in length and about 0.5 mile wide at its entrance.

Approach The entrance is between Rubha Bhalamuis Bhig with rocks extending 100m offshore on the E side, and Aird a'Bhaigh on the W side from which a series of above and below water rocks extends 4 cables SE'wards terminating in Pender Rock (with 0.3m over it). The tidal streams run strongly near Pender Rock resulting in substantial turbulence and should be avoided. There are two rocks which dry about 3.0m, lying 0.5 cable W of Sgeir Niogaig, a 5m high rock, which is close off the NE shore, 5 cables WNW of Rubha Bhalamuis Bhig (see plan below). From the S and E the loch should be well open before entering; then keep about 2 cables off the E shore

Anchorage **Eilean Thinngarstaigh** on the E side 1 mile within the loch (see photograph on p. 79). Pass W and N of the island and anchor on the E side of the island in 8m, mud and sand. Good shelter reported in S'ly and W'ly gales. Some swell probably enters with S'ly winds.

Tob Smuaisibhig about 2.5 miles within the loch on the E side. Good holding in the bay as far into the inlet as depth will allow. A considerable sea sets in during S'ly gales.

Goban Rainich, an inlet on the W side 1 mile within the loch provides shelter from the SW'ly gales. With weather from the S or SE the anchorage behind Eilean Thinngarstaigh would be preferred.

Loch Valamus (Bhalamuis)

Chart (ii) 1794 North Minch (Southern Part)

Tides Const. —0027 Ullapool (—0447 Dover)
MHWS 5.0 MHWN 3.7 ML 2.9
MLWN 2.1 MLWS 0.8

General A small inlet running about 0.5 mile N'wards between Rubha Bhalamuis Bhig, the E entrance point to Loch Claidh, and Rubha a'Bhaird, the W entrance point to Loch Bhrollum.

Approach From the E keep at least 3 cables offshore with Rubha Bhalamuis Bhig on the W side of the entrance bearing not less than 250°, until the loch is well open. This will avoid reefs Sgeir nan Sgarbh and Sgeir Mhor Bhalamuis extending 2 cables from the shore E of the entrance. When within the loch hold well to the W side to avoid drying rocks on the E side.

Anchorage Anchor near the head of the loch just beyond the promontory on the E shore clear of the shallows, isolated rocks and drying area indicated on the plan.

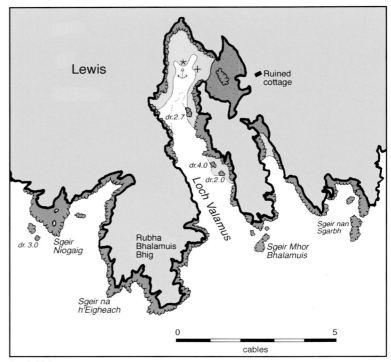

Loch Valamus

Loch Bhrollum

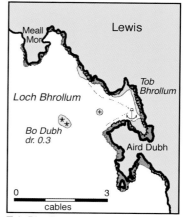

Tob Bhrollum

Tides
Const. —0027 Ullapool (—0447 Dover)
MHWS 5.0   MHWN 3.7   ML 2.9   MLWN 2.1   MLWS 0.8

General
Extending 2 miles into this desolate mountainous region of Lewis, Loch Bhrollum may be visited whilst awaiting the tide to make passage N round Rubh'Uisenis or when planning to visit the Shiant Islands.

The entrance to Loch Bhrollum is between bold headlands, Rubha a'Bhaird and Rubha Bhrollum. The entrance is about 5 cables wide and is free of danger to within 0.5 cables of each shore. The loch extends 2 miles N and its entrance is about 2 miles E of the entrance to Loch Claidh and 2 miles W of Rubha'Uisenis.

Approach
Keep at least a cable from either shore at the entrance to avoid rocks. Once within the loch there are no hidden dangers until Aird Dubh (15m), a grassy peninsula on the E side, 6 cables from the loch entrance.

Anchorage
Tob Bhrollum N of Aird Dubh. Pass Aird Dubh keeping just 60m offshore to avoid two rocks off the N end of Aird Dubh, namely Bogha Dubh (dr 0.3m) 1 cable NW, and another with 0.3m over it 0.5 cable N. Some swell enters with S'ly winds but the effects may be reduced by moving further into the SE corner. Good holding in 4 to 6m.

Head of the Loch. The loch narrows to a cable N of Meall Mor, the headland on the E side of the loch, N of Tob Bhrollum. There are no hazards on either shore except for an isolated rock close to the E shore opposite the island at the head of the loch. Leave the island to port. Depths gradually decrease to 1.2m just N of the island but the bottom is soft mud and yachts sink in without listing. There appears to be good shelter especially behind the island. It is used by fishermen in bad weather. Anchor clear of the rocks reported to be about 50m N of the island.

Loch Bhrollum anchorage   Edward Mason

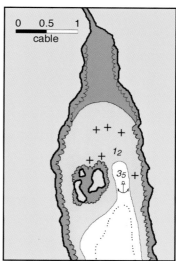

Head of Loch Bhrollum

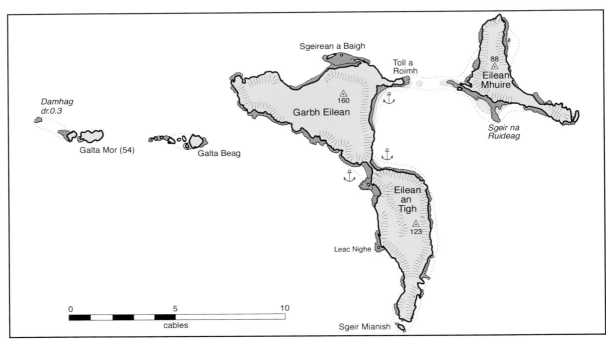

Shiant Islands

Shiant Islands

Charts

(ii) 1795 The little Minch
(ii) 1794 North Minch (Southern Part)
OS 14

General

The Shiant Islands lie about 5 miles E of the entrance to Loch Bhrollum. They are usually uninhabited except for sheep and a profusion of seabirds. Set in tidal swirls S of the often turbulent **Sound of Shiant** (see p. 76 for Caution), the islands may be visited in suitable weather conditions but provide only temporary anchorage.

There are three islands, Garbh Eilean, Eilean Mhuire and Eilean an Tighe. Garbh Eilean, joined to Eilean an Tighe, has higher cliffs than Eilean an Tighe but the latter's are more precipitous. There are 2 islets and a drying rock, Galta Beag, Galta Mor (54m) with Damhag (dr 0.3m) extending in a line over 1 mile W from the NW end of Garbh Eilean.

There is a passage about 3 cables wide between Galta Beag and the W side of Garbh Eilean, and also a passage between Eilean Mhuire and the E side of Garbh Eilean. Both may be used in suitable conditions.

Tides

E of the Shiant Islands
S-going stream begins +0305 Ullapool (—0115 Dover) and turns SW south of the islands. Spring rate 2 knots.
NE-going stream begins —0320 Ullapool (+0445 Dover) but is rather uncertain.
Slack water +0150 Ullapool (—0230 Dover) until the S-going stream begins again.

Note: For tides in the **Sound of Shiant W of the Islands** see p. 76

S of the Shiant Islands up to a distance of 1 mile the streams run ENE and WSW and reach a spring rate in each direction of 3 knots. There are heavy overfalls during the E-going stream.

South Shiant Rock with 5m over it lies 2.5 miles S of Galta mor (54m). The streams near this rock are more or less rotatory, the timing being as follows :—
At +0150 Ullapool (—0230 Dover) the stream is weak, running SSE and changing direction gradually to W as the rate increases.
At +0505 Ullapool (—0045 Dover) the stream runs strongly WSW gradually turning through W and N and then ENE. The spring rate in WSW and ENE directions is 3 knots but more over the rock.

Approach

From the N pass between Garbh Eilean and Eilean Mhuire. This passage is restricted by a drying reef and a sunken rock extending 1.5 cables W from Eilean Mhuire and a sand spit extending 0.5 cable from Garbh Eilean. Keep slightly W of mid-channel. The tide can reach 3 knots.

From the S, approaching the E sides of Eilean an Tighe and Garbh Eilean is straightforward but note the reef extending 1.5 cables from Eilean Mhuire from the middle of the S side.

Anchorage

On the E side of a gravel spit between Garbh Eilean and Eilean an Tighe. Exposed NE-SE. A heavy swell sets in with SW winds, but it is sheltered from winds from the N through W to S. It is reported that in settled weather there is good holding in the sand in 10m in the little bay in the NE corner of Garbh Eilean on the S side of Toll a'Roimh and the natural arch. It is also possible in very favourable weather conditions to anchor off the W side of the spit joining Eilean an Tighe to Garbh Eilean. (see photograph opposite)

Eastern anchorage, Shiant Islands

Charles Tait

Western anchorage, Shiant Islands

Pat and Jill Barron

Loch Seaforth looking SE from above Aline Lodge (p. 79)

Charles Tait

Camus Orasaidh, Loch Erisort with Loch Mariveg beyond (pp. 88 - 91)

Jane Routh

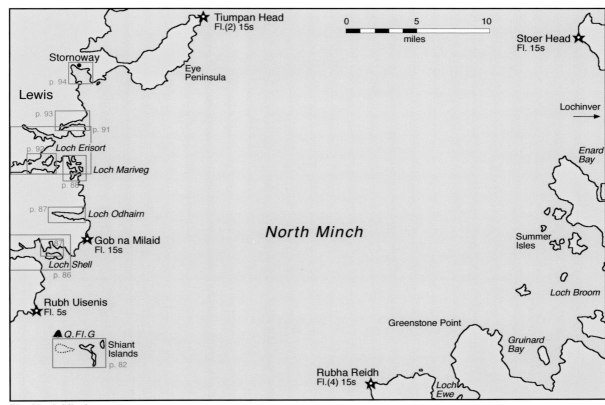

The North Minch

Crossing the North Minch

Chart
(ii) 1794 North Minch, Southern Part
(ii) 1785 North Minch, Northern Part

General
The distances for the crossing of the North Minch are considerably greater than across the Little Minch but, although much exposed to the weather and swell which is present on strong N'ly winds, tidal considerations are significantly less.

Tides

In the southern part of the North Minch
S-going streams begin +0410 Ullapool (HW Dover)
N-going streams begin —0150 Ullapool (—0600 Dover)

In the northern part of the North Minch
S-going streams begin +0510 Ullapool (+0100 Dover)
N-going streams begin —0050 Ullapool (—0500 Dover)

The mean spring rate offshore is between 0.5 and 1 knot with stronger streams occurring at headlands and particularly in the vicinity of the Shiant Islands (see p. 82).

Principal Lights

Mainland
Rubha Reidh   Fl (4).15s 37m 24M. Wh twr
Stoer Head   Fl.15s 59m 24M   Wh twr
Cape Wrath   Fl (4). 30s 122m 22M Wh twr
Scalpay, Harris
Eilean Glas   Fl (3).20s 43m 23M Wh twr red bands
North Skye
Eilean Trodday Fl (2). WRG10s 52m12-9M. Wh framework twr
South Rona   Fl.12s 69m 19M.   Wh twr

Lewis
Butt of Lewis   Fl.5s 52m 25M.   Red brick twr
Tiumpan Head Fl (2).15s 55m 25M Wh twr
Gob na Milaid Fl.15s 17m 10M.   Wh framework twr
Rubh 'Uisenis Fl.5s 24m 11M.   Wh twr

Distances
From South Rona (Acarseid Mhor) to Tob Lemreway (Loch Shell) 33 miles, to Stornoway 47 miles
From N of Skye to Tob Lemreway (Loch Shell) passing E of the Shiant Islands 20 miles
From Badachro (Gairloch) to Tob Lemreway (Loch Shell) 30 miles, to Stornoway 38 miles
From Camus Angus (Loch Ewe) to Tob Lemreway (Loch Shell) 40 miles, to Stornoway 33 miles
From Loch Inver to Tob Lemreway (Loch Shell) 40 miles, to Stornoway 37 miles
From Kinlochbervie to Tob Lemreway (Loch Shell) 51 miles, to Stornoway 47 miles

Landfalls
Loch Shell (Isle of Lewis) offers good protection particularly in Tob Lemreway. It is easy of access in all conditions and makes an intermediate point of arrival at the Outer Hebrides between East Loch Tarbert, Harris and Stornoway. From the E a large vertical mark near Rubha Ailltenish, the S entrance point, can be seen from well out to sea.

Stornoway. The approach from the S is straightforward but from the E the notorious Chicken Rock (5m high), where a troop ship returning after the end of the 1914 -18 War was wrecked with the tragic loss of many lives, lies 3.5 miles E of the harbour entrance. It is marked by a south cardinal buoy Q (6) + LFl.15s. The harbour itself is easy of access in all conditions. Full details are given on pp. 93, 94 & 95.

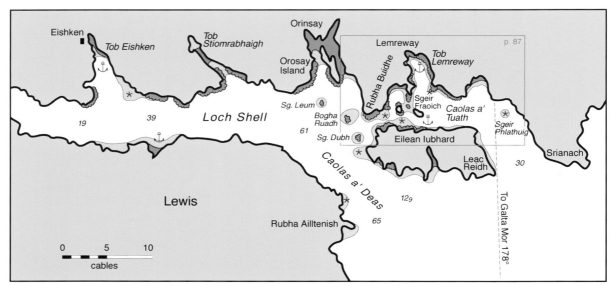

Loch Shell

Loch Shell (Loch Sealg)

Chart
(ii) 1794 North Minch, Southern Part
OS 14

General
Loch Shell is one of the best and most convenient anchorages on the E coast of Lewis. Its prominent danger-free entrance is easy of access and the Loch itself provides good shelter. For those making passage in the North Minch it makes a convenient place of arrival at the Outer Hebrides being about mid-way between Stornoway, Lewis and East Loch Tarbert, Harris; and N of the Shiant Islands and the strong tides in the Sound of Shiant.

The entrance to the loch is between Rubha Ailltenish on the S side and Srianach, a bold headland with a vertical face on the NE side. From Srianach to the head of the loch is 6 miles and to Tob Eishken about 4 miles. The S shore which leads to the inner loch, given a reasonable offing, is free from hazard. The N shore has many indentations which provide some well protected anchorages particularly those in Caolas a'Tuath off the N shore of Eilean Iubhard, and in the inlet of Tob Lemreway.

Tides
Streams in Loch Shell are barely perceptible.
Const. —0016 Ullapool (—0436 Dover) MHWS 4.8   MHWN 3.6   ML 2.8   MLWN 1.9   MLWS 0.7

Tob Lemreway

General
Whereas there are reefs and drying rocks W and N of Eilean Iubhard, Caolas a'Tuath provides a clear approach to Tob Lemreway. In W'ly gales Caolas a'Tuath is subject to very violent gusts.

Approach
From the S the long low finger of Leac Reidh, the SE corner of Eilean Iubhard may be distinguished against the much higher background of the Lewis shore. The entrance to Caolas a'Tuath is between Leac Reidh and Srianach. Note Sgeir Phlathuig (dr 0.6m) 1 cable from the N shore. This rock is off a ravine with large boulders at the mouth where the shore line changes from cliffs to steep hills. The SE point of Eilean Iubhard in line with Galta Mor (Shiant Islands) bearing 178° astern leads W of Sgeir Phlathuig. Sron Chrom, the NE point of Eilean Iubhard in line with Rubha Buidhe leads S of it.
As reefs, terminating in a drying rock, extend more than 0.5 cable off the E shore at the entrance to Tob Lemreway, head towards Sgeir Fraoich till the entrance is well open. Once within Tob Lemreway keep at least 0.5 cable off both shores and note that there are drying rocks lying offshore 2 cables from the head of the inlet. (see plan p. 87).

Anchorage **Off the pier** clear of small boat moorings on the W side towards the head of the inlet. Note the position of the rocks from the plan. Good holding but subject to squalls from the N.
NW of the E point of the entrance to the Tob Lemreway inlet is recommended.
Off the N shore of Eilean Iubhard provides more shelter in fresh to strong S'ly winds. Anchor close in on a shallow ledge W of the fish cages. In SE winds this may be subject to swell.
NW of Sgeir Ghlas provides alternative shelter in SE winds although it is deep (15m). If making passage westwards from Caolas a Tuath hold closer to Sgeir Fraoich and Sgeir Ghlas to avoid the rocks off Eilean Iubhard but take note of the reef which stretches S from Sgeir Ghlas. The NW side of Eilean Iubhard is rock strewn and obstructed by fish farm equipment and is not suitable for anchoring.

Facilities
Water at pier. Tel. P.O.

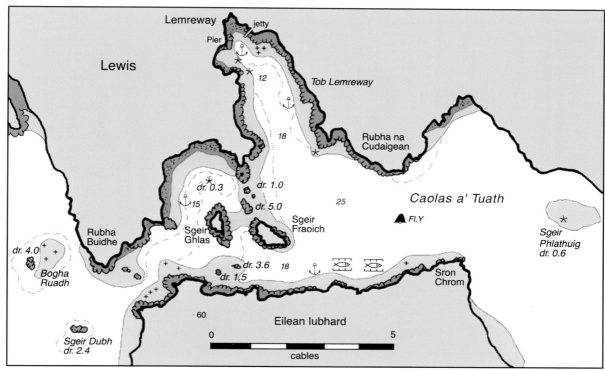

Tob Lemreway

Inner Loch Shell

Approach Enter S of Eilean Iubhard and, when past that island, its SW side should bear no more than 120° astern to clear rocks W of the island. The S shore is clean above Rubha Ailltenish.

Anchorage **Tob Eishken.** This inlet lies on the N side of the loch 2.5 miles W of Eilean Iubhard. Note the drying rock lying 1 cable off the NE shore of the entrance and a rock awash 0.25 cable from the W side 2 cables S of Eishken Lodge. The anchorage is at the head of the inlet but is reported foul with lost moorings.

SE of Tob Eishken the bight on the S shore is sheltered from S'ly winds. The beach dries off considerably.

The Head of the Loch is clear and suitable for anchorage but dries out for about 2 cables. It is sheltered except from the E.

Loch Odhairn

General Immediately N of Kebock Head this loch is free from dangers and swell seldom reaches the head. The loch runs inland for 2 miles.

Tides Const.—0016 Ullapool (—0436 Dover)
MHWS 4.8 MHWN 3.7 ML 2.9 MLWN 2.0
MLWS 0.7

Anchorage In the bay on the S side, opposite the jetty, just before the loch finally narrows. Exposed to the E. In SW gales heavy squalls come down the slopes on the S side.

Facilities P.O. Tel. at Gravir, 1 mile. Water from the well at the cottage near the slip at the jetty.

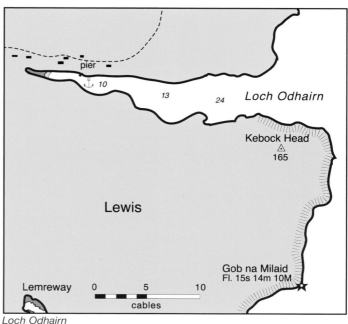

Loch Odhairn

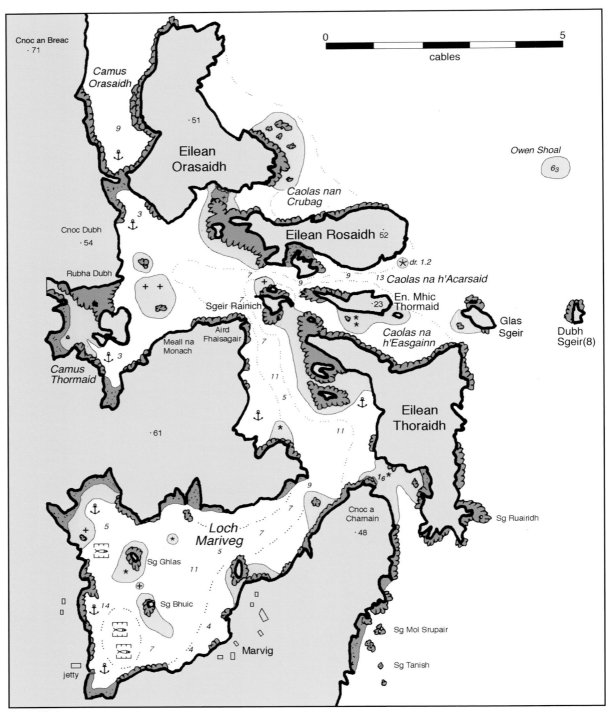

Loch Mariveg

Loch Mariveg (Mharabhig)

Charts	(ii)	1794 North Minch, Southern Part
	(iii)	2529 Approaches to Stornoway OS 14

Tides   Const.—0010 Ullapool (—0430 Dover)   MHWS 4.8   MHWN 3.7   ML 2.9   MLWN 2.0   MLWS 0.7

General   Lying about 6 miles S of Stornoway Harbour there are two indentations in the coastline on the SE side of the entrance to Loch Erisort which have their entrances almost completely enclosed by three islands and a number of islets. This results in a network of sheltered bays giving a surprising variety of sheltered anchorages.

Loch Mariveg is sheltered by Eilean Thoraidh. N of the entrances to Loch Mariveg, Eilean Orasaidh and Eilean Rosaidh provide sheltered anchorages on each side of the drying bar S of Camus Orasaidh.

There are two entrances to Loch Mariveg, one to the S between Cnoc a'Charnain and Eilean Thoraidh and the other, Caolas na h'Acarsaid, 3 cables WNW of Dubh Sgeir (8m), between Eilean Rosaidh and Eilean Mhic Thoraidh. Both entrance passages are narrow. The entrances may be dangerous to enter in fresh to strong E'ly winds.

Approach

The S'ly channel S of Eilean Thoraidh has only 1.6m but it is the wider entrance. It would be unwise to attempt this passage below half tide. Keep SW of mid-channel to avoid a drying rock in the narrows. The E end of the islet W of Eilean Thoraidh open of the SW point of Eilean Thoraidh clears this rock. This line should be identified before entering the channel. Note: At the W end of the channel a reef extends 50m from the N point of Cnoc a'Charnain.

Caolas na h'Acarsaid, the N'ly channel immediately S of Eilean Rosaidh, although narrow, is less obstructed than the S channel and has greater depth. The rock SE of Eilean Rosaidh (dr. 1.2m) may be dangerous if a swell is running. Give the NW end of Sgeir Rainich a berth of 0.5 cable to clear the reef off it before heading for the anchorages within the loch.

Once through either of the entrances steer to avoid a reef off the NW shore of Cnoc a'Charnain and keep nearer to the NW shore. Maintain this course until Loch Mariveg is well open. Within the loch note the awash rock about 1 cable ENE of Sgeir Ghlas and another about 0.5 cable SW of that islet. There are two more rocks side by side 1 cable WNW of Sgeir Glas. There is also a rock between Sgeir Glas and Sgeir Bhuic.

Anchorage

Loch Mariveg, as convenient for wind direction. The SW corner is reported foul with heavy chain. The jetty in the SW corner is tidal.

Eilean Thoraidh. In the bay on the W side of the island in 4m. Rocks extend SE from the S'ly islet.

Aird Fhalasgeir. In the bay S of the of point in 3.5m. Note the rock on the S side of the bay.

Camus Thormaid. In the approach keep 30m off the Meall na Monach shore to avoid a drying rock to the N. Anchor in 3m SW of the islet. Note that the pool W of the islet shoals rapidly and is full of weed.

Facilities

P.O. Tel. at Marvig. Mobile shop weekdays.

Camus Thormaid, Loch Mariveg   *Edward Mason*

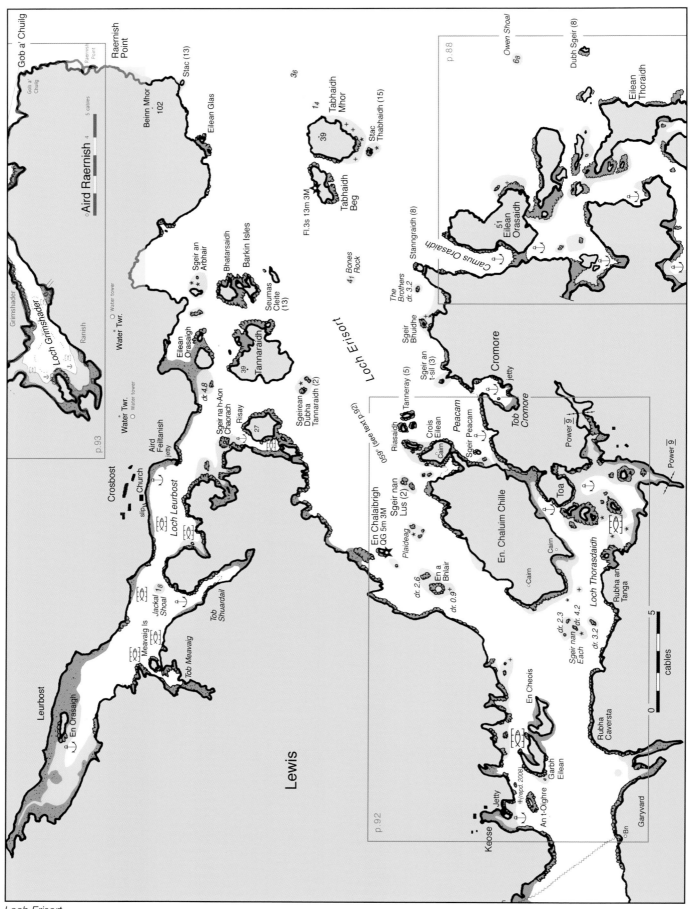

Loch Erisort

Loch Erisort

Charts
(ii) 1794 North Minch (Southern Part)
(iii) 2529 Approaches to Stornoway
OS 14

Tides
Const. —0010 Ullapool (—0430 Dover) MHWS 4.8 MHWN 3.7 ML 2.9 MLWN 2.9 MLWS 0.7
In-going stream begins —0610 Ullapool (+0200 Dover)
Out-going stream begins +0005 Ullapool (—0415 Dover)
The streams are barely perceptible except in the narrow channels.

Lights
Tabhaidh Bheag	Fl 3s 13m 3M	Concrete structure. (The light is obscured from the E)
Eilean Chalaibrigh	QG 5m 3M	Concrete structure.

General
Loch Erisort, whose entrance is a little over a mile wide, runs W'wards for 9 miles, 7 miles of which are navigable. This is a well inhabited part of Lewis. The S side of the loch entrance has some sheltered anchorages which are easy to enter. The N side of the entrance leads to Loch Leurbost, an arm of the sea reaching 2.5 miles NW which is well sheltered from all directions.

Within Loch Erisort itself there are many islets, reefs and rocks, but with the use of Chart 2529, all dangers may be avoided. All rocks show at LW except Bones Rock (depth 4m) in the outer part of Loch Erisort and Jackal Shoal (depth 1.8m) in Loch Leurbost.

Tabhaidh Mhor and Tabhaidh Bheag are islands which lie in the centre of the approach to the loch. Barkin Isles, with the castellated quarried Seumas Cleite (13) and Tannaraidh to the W, shelter the entrance to Loch Leurbost. A large island, Eilean Chaluim Chille joined to the S Lewis shore at LW, narrows Loch Erisort considerably. The inner loch is entered N of this island. **Caution.** Keep a sharp lookout for nets in all parts of the loch.

Approach
From the S Owen Shoal (with 6.8 over it) lies 3 cables N of Dubh Sgeir (8m) near the entrance to Loch Mariveg. If making for Peacam, pass between Bones Rock (with 4.1m over it) and The Brothers (dr. 3.2m) 1 cable W of Stanngraidh.

From the N or E the approach is straightforward as Tabhaidh Bheag and Tabhaidh Mhor can be passed on either hand but beware a shoal patch (LD 1.4m) 150m off the NE side of Tabhaidh Mhor and a further patch (LD 3.6) approximately 3c off. Note also Bones Rock (LD 4.1).
If making for Loch Leurbost the straightforward approach is between the W side of Tannaraidh and Sgeirean Dubh Tannaraidh (2). Keep closer to the SW end of Tannaraidh to avoid reefs to port.

Anchorage
In Outer Loch Erisort
Camas Orasaidh lies S of Stanngraidh on the W side of Eilean Orasaidh. Hold well over to the W side of the bay on entry as rocks extend 40m off the E shore. Good holding in mud. Exceptionally this bay is subject to swell in N'ly winds or E'ly gales. It is said that when The Brothers (dr. 3.2m) (see above) are covered, a small vessel can make passage S from the head of Camus Orasaidh into the N basin of Loch Mariveg. Keep to the E side of the narrows.

Peacam (Cromore Bay). From Rubha Stanngraidh keep 1.5 cable offshore to avoid The Brothers (dr 3.2m) and leave the above water rocks, Sgeir Bhuidhe and Sgeir an t-sil (3m) to port. Anchor in 4m S of Sgeir Peacam.

Tob Cromore. A shallow pool with a cable wide entrance on the SE side of Peacam. Clay bottom, shoal towards the head. Note the drying rock 0.3 cable from the NW shore. Anchor as soon as the pool opens out in 2.5m.

Facilities
Tel. at Cromore.

Loch Leurbost

Approach
Loch Leurbost is best entered SW of Tannaraidh, keeping close to that island to avoid drying rocks E of Sgeirean Dubh Tannaraidh. After passing W of Tannaraidh head round to port to enter the loch. Entry can also be made N of Barkin Isles and Tannaraidh. Note the rock (dr 4.8m) which lies 1 cable W of Eilean Orasaigh on the N shore. This rock rarely covers.

Anchorage
Near the Head of the Loch, not much beyond Orasaigh, in 3m mud.

Tob Shuardail Note Jackal Shoal (1.8m over it) at the E side of the entrance. Anchor in 2.5m as far within the inlet as depth and size allow.

Crosbost Anchor clear of moorings in the wide bay between the church and the jetty on Aird Feiltanish.

Facilities
Crosbost; PO, tel.

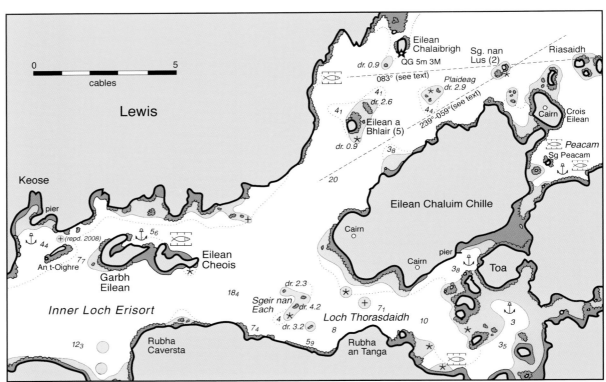

Entrance to Inner Loch Erisort and Loch Thorasdaidh

Inner Loch Erisort

Approach The entrance to the Inner Loch requires special care as a large reef, Plaideag (dr 2.9m), lies in the centre. The principal entrance passage is S of Plaideag and should be approached S of Sgeir nan Lus (2) on a course equidistant from Sgeir nan Lus and the N point of Eilean Chalium Chille. Thereafter a course of approximately 239° will leave Plaideag to starboard. A useful clearance bearing for avoiding Plaideag both when entering and leaving the Inner Loch is to keep the N entrance point of Loch Erisort just open of Sgeir na Lus on a bearing of 059°.

When leaving the Inner Loch there is a useful and straightforward route passing W of Eilean a Bhlair and then making for the channel N of Eilean Chalaibrigh. Although the channel is narrow the passage through presents no difficulty. This passage in certain conditions may be the preferred route for entering the Inner Loch.

Caution. Beware of the rock (dr 0.9m) lying half a cable SW of Eilean Chalaibrigh. If deciding to pass S of En. Chalaibrigh a transit of 083° with Sgeir nan Lus in line with the N side of Riasaidh clears this rock and the reefs (dr 2.6m) NE of Eilean a Bhlair.

Anchorage **Keose** Enter to the W of An t-Oighre to avoid the rock (reported 2008) in the channel to the N of the island. Anchor S of the jetty in 3m, soft mud. Beware of the rock close inshore E of the jetty. Or anchor N of Garbh Eilean.

Loch Thorasdaidh (Hurista)

Approach With the E side of Eilean Cheois astern, head for the W end of the bay W of Rubh'an Tanga, steering approximately SE. Keep 30m off the S shore until well into the bay leaving to port the many drying reefs off Eilean Chaluim Chille which extend to within almost half a cable of the S shore. Follow round the shore 30 to 50m off from Rubh'an Tanga until through the narrows and into the loch.

Anchorage Between the **W side of Toa and the jetty** on the E side of Eilean Chaluim Chille. Good holding in mud. **Alternatively** pass S of the most S'ly islet in the middle of the S corner of the loch and anchor 1 cable NE of it in 3m. Some swell sets in with strong W or NW winds.

Loch Grimshader

General The head of this loch provides perfect shelter as does Loch Beag, a spur extending 5 cables NW, although the latter is obstructed by a power cable (see plan and text opposite). At the entrance to Loch Grimshader there is, on the edge of the cliff on the S side of the entrance, a remarkable rock having the appearance of a lion's head.

Tide Const. —0010 Ullapool (—0430 Dover) MHWS 4.8 MHWN 3.7 ML 2.9 MLWN 2.9 MLWS 0.7

Approach From the N give Sgeir Linish, an above water rock, a wide berth to avoid extending reefs. Sgeir a'Chaolais (dr 3.7m) lies 5 cables within the entrance and when the S point of the entrance is kept in sight this leads N of it. After passing that rock hold to the south shore to avoid rock lying off the N shore. The depth decreases rapidly after passing Sgeir a'Chaolais.

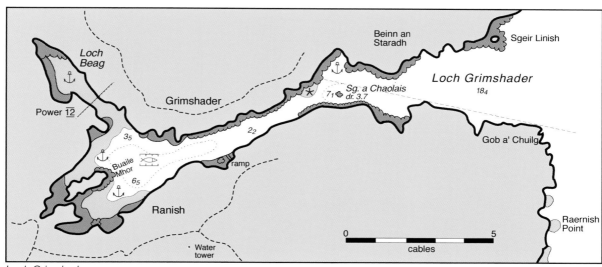

Loch Grimshader

Loch Grimshader (continued)

Anchorage **The bay N of Sgeir a'Chaolais** is reported as quite a good anchorage.
Head of the Loch in bays either side of Buaile Mhor.
Loch Beag can be approached by keeping to the NE side of a very narrow channel, 3m deep, with rocks on SW side. An overhead Power Cable crosses this channel with a clearance of 12m at HW. The tidal stream in the narrows is 2 to 3 knots. Anchor off the burn on the NW side in 4m mud. This anchorage is reported to be silting.

Facilities PO, tel. at Crosbost (see plan p. 90). PO at Grimshader on the N side of the loch.

Stornoway, Cromwell St. quay pontoons   *Arthur Houston*

Stornoway

Charts (ii) 1785 North Minch, Northern Part
(ii) 1794 North Minch, Southern Part
(iii) 2529 Approaches to Stornoway and Stornoway Harbour
OS 8

General Stornoway Harbour is the largest harbour in the Hebrides. It is very sheltered and easy to enter at all states of the tide. With the largest concentration of population in the Western Isles, Stornoway has many facilities in contrast to other parts of the islands. It is 30 miles from the Butt of Lewis to Stornoway Harbour. The Eye Peninsula, E of Stornoway Harbour, is low lying and looks like an island when viewed from some distance off.

Tide Const. —0010 Ullapool (—0430 Dover) MHWS 4.8   MHWN 3.7   ML 2.9   MLWN 2.0   MLWS 0.7
Streams are negligible in the harbour and approaches.

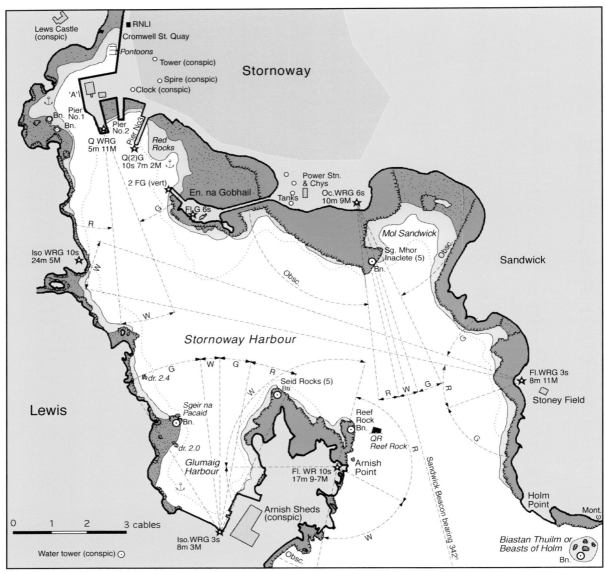

Stornoway and approaches

Stornoway (continued)

Lights

Approach from the East

Chicken Rock (beacon)	Q(6)+LFl.15s	S Cardinal pillar Lt buoy
Nato Fuel Jetty (Branahie Bay)	2 F.R. (vert) 11m 6M	Metal column

Harbour Entrance and Approach lights
On or near W shore

Arnish Point	Fl.WR.10s 17m 9/7M	Wh Round Twr (W sector 102°—109° (7°))
Reef Rock	Q.R.	Red can light buoy
Glumaig Harbour	Iso.WRG 3s 8m 3M	Metal pole
Greeta Light	Iso.WRG 10s 24m 5M	Metal pole

On E shore

Stoney Field	Fl.WRG. 3s 8m.	Metal pole

On N shore

Sandwick Bay	Oc.WRG.6s 10m 9M	Metal pole (W sector 341°—347° (6°))

Inner Harbour Lights

Eilean na Gobhail, N shore	Fl.G.6s 8m.	Metal column
Slipway nearby	2F.G (vert)	Concrete column
No 1 Pier (former Ro-Ro terminal)	Q.WRG. 5m 11M.	Pole (W sector 335°—352° (17°))
No 3 Pier - New Ro-Ro Terminal	Q(2).G.10s 7m 2M	Column

Marks   Sandwick Beacon, 5 metres high, on Sg. Mhor Inaclete.
3 grey chimneys of the Power Station on Inaclete Point on the N side of the harbour.
Arnish Sheds, very conspicuous, on the W side of the harbour entrance.
Memorial Tower on Holm Point seen against the skyline on the E side of the harbour entrance.

Stornoway (continued)

Approach This is straightforward with the Sandwick Beacon on the N shore on Sgeir Mhor Inaclete bearing 342°. Follow round to port in the centre of the fairway. The hazards off the NE and N shore of Arnish Point are marked by a red can light buoy QR and an unlit beacon. Keep a look out for fishing boats and the large ferry using this busy harbour. At night keep in the white sector of each of three sectored lights in turn (see above). Continue past pier No.1 and into the inner harbour. Call the Harbour Office, call sign "Stornoway Harbour" on Channel 12, for berthing instructions.

Berthing **Pontoons** (depth 2.5m) with berths for visitors are positioned at Cromwell Street Quay. Water at pontoons. There are no visitors moorings. Use of the pontoons is preferable to anchoring. Report to the Harbour Office (during normal working hours, or the Harbour Watchroom on Esplanade Quay - near letter 'A' on plan) to obtain keycard for shore access to the pontoons. Alternatively tie up alongside Cromwell Street Quay and contact Harbour Office (tel: 01851 702688). Avoid berthing on fishing vessels which leave early.
Esplanade Quay. At approximately the position of letter 'A' on plan weather boarding is available.

Anchorage **Port nam Portan** on the W side of the harbour opposite the Esplanade Quay (letter 'A' on plan) provides limited anchoring space due to moorings of local boats. Anchor N of the beacons and avoid swinging into the fairway. Holding is reported as poor.
Eilean na Gobhail. Anchor in the bay NW of the island. Keep well clear of No 3 Pier. The Ro-Ro terminal is on the W side of the pier. Note shoal water and drying rocks inshore. Warning: near HW in S'ly winds waves are reflected by the sea wall along the beach. This makes the area quite turbulent.
Glumaig Harbour. Reefs extend 2 cables N of Arnish Point and 1.5 cable E'wards from the W side of the entrance. Both are both marked by beacons. Oil and steel industry construction works have been established with piers and foreshore works. Debris has recently been cleared from the sea bed but a strong tripping line is still recommended.

Facilities **The Harbour Office** (tel 01851 702688) has a full list of technical repair and other services, including information for obtaining marine diesel (key card needed, see p.5). Water hose on wall at fish market (inner harbour), also at hydrant at No.1 pier. Obtain hydrant key from the Harbour Office.
Shops, super market, P.O. and Tel. Chandlery. **Hospital** (tel. 01851 704704). Petrol and Calor gas. **Tourist Information Centre** (tel. 01851 703088) at 4 South Beach Street. Yachtsmen are welcome to use the Seamen's Mission, cafeteria and showers. Swimming Pool and showers at Nicolson Sports Centre. Car hire and taxi services.
Daily car ferry to Ullapool by **Caledonian MacBrayne** (tel 01851 702361). Air service to Glasgow and Inverness, and inter-island air services by **British Airways** (tel. 01851 703673).
R.N.L.I. Lifeboat Station.
Coastguard MRSC at Battery Point (tel. 01851 702013). (See also Introduction p. 5).
Customs. There is no customs office at Stornoway. For clearance contact the office at Aberdeen (Tel 01224 844610; fax 01224 644610).
Western Isles Council is responsible, except for Stornoway, for all piers, pontoons and moorings for visitors throughout the Outer Hebrides. Contact their Harbour Master (tel. 01851 703773 or 01870 602425).

Activities Hire a car or taxi and visit Callanish Stone Circles and Standing Stones; also two other stone circles nearby and Dun Carloway Broch on NE side of Loch Roag. St Columba's Church at Eye is the burial place of the MacLeods of Lewis.

Stornoway to Butt of Lewis

Charts (ii) 1785 North Minch (Northern Part)
(iii) 2529 Approaches to Stornoway

Lights

Chicken Rock (beacon)	Q(6)+LFl.15s	S Cardinal pillar Lt buoy
Tiumpan Head	Fl (2) 15s 55m 25M	Wh. twr.
Butt of Lewis Lt Ho	Fl 5s 52m 25M	Red brick twr.

Passage There is little shelter between Stornoway and the Butt of Lewis apart from Port of Ness (see below). The passage round the Butt of Lewis is hazardous due to strong tidal streams. **Details of the strength and direction of the tide are given on p. 108** In addition to the tide there is exposure to the wind and heavy swell from most directions which can make the Butt of Lewis more dangerous to round than Cape Wrath. Small vessels should keep at least 5 miles off except in very settled conditions. **In no circumstances should the Butt of Lewis be approached when white water is seen off it.**

Anchorage **Port of Ness** A couple of miles S of the Butt of Lewis. A shallow indentation with sandy bottom provides good holding ground but is only suitable in offshore winds. Subject to swell. The harbour is silted up but boats drawing up to 1.6m can enter at HW and dry out, but even the harbour is subject to swell.

West Coasts of the Uists and Benbecula

Charts (i) 2722 Skerryvore to St Kilda
(i) 2721 St Kilda to Butt of Lewis
OS 22

Lights Monach Isles   Fl (2) 15s 19m 10M   Wh framework Twr
Vallay (Griminish Harbour) Fl WRG 3s 4m 8M   Column on wh base
Haskeir Island   Fl 20s 44m 23M   Wh Twr (Racon 'M')
South Uist Firing Range - see below under Danger Areas

General The W coasts of South Uist, Benbecula and North Uist are low lying and lacking in distinctive features. There are many rocks, reefs and shoal patches lying within 3 miles of the shore which cause heavy breaking seas in strong W'ly winds. There is no secure shelter between Barra Head and the Sound of Harris. **Note:** There are many lines of lobster pots laid offshore which are poorly marked or not marked at all.

Tides S of the Monach Islands
N-going stream begins —0420 Ullapool (+0345 Dover)
S-going stream begins +0205 Ullapool (—0215 Dover)
The tides are under 0.5 knot at springs and offshore but gain strength as the shallower water round the islands is approached. The tide runs strongly both E and W of the Monach Islands.

Passage Making passage N from the Sound of Barra keeping at least 3 to 4 miles offshore will clear all hazards until Bo Ruag (dr 1.2m), generally marked by breakers, is reached. This dangerous rock lies 3 miles W of Balivanich, Benbecula. From Northbay, Barra to the Monach Islands is about 36 miles.

Danger Areas. Weapon firing areas extends up to 100 miles NW of South Uist. A "clear range" policy is maintained. The majority of range activity (90%) takes place within an inshore danger area extending about 30 miles NW and SW from Ardivachar Point. **Lights** are exhibited near this point and at Rubha Ardvule before and during firing periods. These comprise Range FR danger lights visible 6/8M which are shown 1 hr before firing takes place and which change to Iso R 2s 15 mins before firing until completion of firing. These lights are also shown during daylight firing and may be seen from 3M away. Radar sea surveillance is maintained when the range is active, with range safety craft patrolling the inner danger zone. All vessels are warned that various pyrotechnic devices may be sighted in or near the range, including rocket motor flares at high altitude, visible at great distances.

Radio information of range activity is broadcast at 1000 daily and 1hr before firing on Ch 73 after an initial alert call on Ch 12. Range control tel. 01870 60 4535/4434/4441. Contact one of these numbers or call on Ch 16 if no broadcast is heard. The range is closed during holiday periods. Stornoway Coast Guard will broadcast a navigational warning whenever the extended 100 mile firing range is to be used.

Monach Islands

Charts (i) 2722 Skerryvore to St Kilda

General This group of five low lying islands, also known as the Heisker Islands, lies about 5 miles offshore in an area of shoals on the W side of North Uist. The lighthouse on Shillay, the most W'ly island, is the most conspicuous mark on the islands. These islands offer anchorage and protection from winds from all directions but undoubtedly should only be visited in settled weather. Great care is needed when in the vicinity of these islands because of the numerous rocks and reefs and tides of up to 2 knots in the channels which surround them. No large scale chart is available.

Light Shillay   Fl(2).15s 47m 18M   Red brick twr.

Tides Const. —0103 Ullapool (—0523 Dover) MHWS 4.2   MHWN 3.0   ML 2.4   MLWN 1.3   MLWS 0.4

In the Sound of Monach
N-going stream begins —0420 Ullapool (+0345 Dover)
S-going stream begins +0205 Ullapool (—0215 Dover)

The streams run strongly both E and W of the islands and in the channels between them and may reach 2 knots at springs in each direction. The N-going streams from E and W of the islands meet 2 miles N of the islands and form an eddy which runs S towards them. Similarly the S-going streams meet 2 miles S of the islands and form an eddy which runs N towards them.

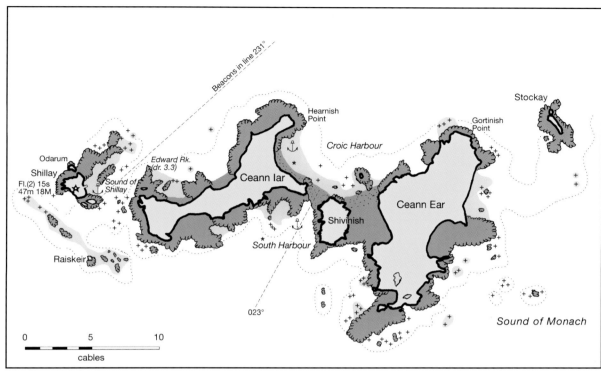

The Monach Islands

Approach **From the S** the approach is straightforward until at least a mile off the Monach Islands. If making for the N side of the Monach Islands pass well W of Huskeiran but note the 5m patch 2 miles W, then enter John's North Channel passing mid-way between Middle Dureberg (dr 2.7m) on the port hand and W Dureberg (dr 1.3m) to starboard. The SW end of the Middle Dureberg can be approached to within 2 cables as, even if covered, it is normally marked by breakers. The N extremity of Stockay in line with Rueval, the highest hill on Benbecula, bearing 116° leads through the fairway until the disused lighthouse bears 204°. Once through John's North Channel the beacons on the E'most islet adjoining Shillay provide a leading line of 231° into the anchorage. The beacons are sometimes not easily seen, especially when entering against the sun.

In clear weather the channel between Huskeiran and Shillay can be taken as the S end of the former always shows. Keep well off the N and NE end of Shillay as reefs extend for over 0.5 mile.

From the N leave the Sound of Harris between Pabbay and Shillay through the Sound of Shillay. Head for a position 2 miles W of Griminish Point. As the approaches to the Monach Islands from Griminish Point have many reefs and rocks, maintain a SW'ly course until the disused lighthouse on Shillay bears 175° then alter course to enter John's North Channel to pass mid-way between Middle Dureberg (dr. 2.7m) on the port hand and W Dureberg (dr 1.2m) to starboard. Follow the leading line of 116° through the fairway and the further directions given above which complete the approach to the Sound of Shillay anchorage.

Alternatively from the N after passing Griminish Point keep 5 cables offshore until Aird an Runair is abeam and then alter to pass through the Sound of Causamul keeping Griminish Point just open of Aird an Runair on a bearing of 029° to clear the Charlotte Rocks. Once past these rocks and with Deasker (3) abeam to starboard course can be altered towards the 40m tall old Monach LH.

Caution. If passing either N'wards or S'wards through the Sound of Monach note particularly East Rock (dr 1.8m) which lies 7.5 cables E of Stockay. Half of Haskeir Island open W of Causamul bearing 333° clears East Rock and Vosgeir (dr 0.6m) which lies 1 mile NNE of East Rock.

Anchorage **Shillay.** Approaching from the N use the two beacons on the E'most islet adjoining the island of Shillay in line bearing 231° to navigate the narrow rock-strewn Sound of Shillay. Under no circumstances approach the anchorage using the S channel. Anchor off the lighthouse jetty in 5m. Good shelter from winds SW to NW.

Croic Harbour. In the approach give Hearnish Point a berth of 2 cables. Anchor on the W side of the bay in 3m between Hearnish and the SE point of Ceann Iar, with the lighthouse bearing not more than 260°, to clear drying rocks in the S half of the bay. There is a strong tidal set inshore on the ebb with SE winds. Good shelter from the SE through S to WNW.

South Harbour. Good shelter in N'ly winds but S'ly scend may be uncomfortable. Approach with the centre of the sandy beach W of Shivinish bearing 023°.

Facilities None

Shillay (Monach Islands) from NW   *Pat and Jill Barron*

West and North Coast of North Uist

Chart   (i) 2722 Skerryvore to St Kilda
               (ii) 2841 Loch Maddy to Loch Resort including the Sound of Harris

General   Between Aird an Runair, the W'most point of N. Uist, and Griminish Point the coast is clear of off-lying rocks but should not be approached closer than 5 cables. From Griminish Point to Berneray there are several dangers, notably Bo Lea which is awash and lies 1.5m N of Valley Island. Inshore of Bo Lea there is a substantial area of reefs extending for 5 cables N'wards from the entrance to Griminish Harbour. The exploration of the N. Uist coast and the offshore islands between Griminish and the Sound of Berneray, now blocked by a causeway between Berneray and N. Uist, can only be achieved with Chart 2841.

Tide   Between Aird an Runair and Griminish Point the streams run in the general direction of the coast. Off Griminish Point the streams are 2 hours earlier than at Monach Islands and at Haskeir.
               N-going stream begins —0605 Ullapool (+0200 Dover)
               S-going stream begins +0020 Ullapool (—0400 Dover)
               The spring rate in each direction is 1 to 1.5 knots off Griminish Point.

Anchorage **Griminish Harbour** is well protected in all conditions behind the W side of Valley Island. However the entrance, about 2 miles E of Griminish Point, is very difficult without local knowledge and cannot be entered at all states of the tide. It would be dangerous to attempt this harbour in bad weather.

               Lingay. Approach on a SE'ly mid-channel course through Caolas a'Mhorain. Be aware of Gairgrada (dr. 1.8m) if approaching from Griminish Point and keep 4 cables off Aird a'Mhorain. Anchor in sand S of the island. Open to the NW but it is reported that little swell is felt.

Sound of Harris to Loch Roag

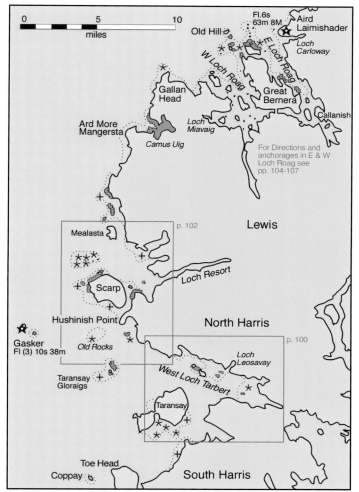

Sound of Harris to Loch Roag

Charts

(i)   2721 St Kilda to the Butt of Lewis
(ii) 2841 Loch Maddy to Loch Resort including the Sound of Harris
(iii) 2515 Ard More Mangersta to Tiumpan including Loch Roag
OS 18, OS 13

Lights

Haskeir: Fl 20s 44m 23M Wh Twr
Gasker: Fl (3) 10s 38m 10M Wh framework Twr.
Flannan Isles: Fl (2) 30s 101m 20M Twr
Aird Laimishader: (N point of East Loch Roag) Fl 6s 63m 8M Wh framework Twr

Tide

E of a line from Griminish Point to Scarp, the tides run as follows :–
N-going stream runs E to the Sound of Harris from +0550 Ullapool (+0130 Dover)
S-going stream runs W from the Sound of Harris from —0020 Ullapool (—0440 Dover)
Away from the salient points or narrow channels the streams are weak.

Between Heisker Islands and Gasker, and along the coast to Gallan Head, the streams run as follows :–
N-going stream begins —0430 Ullapool (+0345 Dover)
S-going stream begins +0155 Ullapool (—0215 Dover)
The streams off Gasker are 2 knots springs in each direction but are weak elsewhere except off salient points.

Passage

Proceeding N from Toe Head the range of mountains of North Harris dominate the skyline with the island of Scarp (306m) at the W extremity of the range. Course should be set towards Gasker (30m) in order to leave the Taransay Glorigs, the highest of which is 12m and the Old Rocks (dr 0.2m and 2.3m) 2.5 miles further N, well to starboard. Hold course until within 2 miles of Gasker when an alteration can be made to pass 1.5 miles W of Scarp which will avoid the rocks 7 cables W of Scarp and the dangerous group of rocks 1.5 miles NNW of Scarp.

Continuing N'wards keeping 1 mile offshore, the radio mast at Ard More Mangersta is conspic. Keep 5 cables off Gallan Head to avoid Sgeir Gallan (dr 3.4m) which lies 3 cables NNW of that headland before altering towards the entrance to West Loch Roag.

Proceeding S to the Sound of Harris. From a position 1 mile off Ard More Mangersta by

Kearstay anchorage, Scarp (see p. 103)   *Pat and Jill Barron*

proceeding on a course for Gasker will clear the dangerous rocks 1.5 miles NNW of Scarp and the further group of rocks W of Scarp. Pass 1.5 miles W of Scarp and when it is abeam course can then be altered for Coppay which lies 1 mile W of Toe Head at the entrance to the Sound of Harris.

Caution

A close watch must be kept to ensure that there is no tendency to wander E of the tracks chosen to avoid the Taransay Glorigs and the Old Rock S of Scarp, and also the dangerous rocks W and NNW of Scarp.

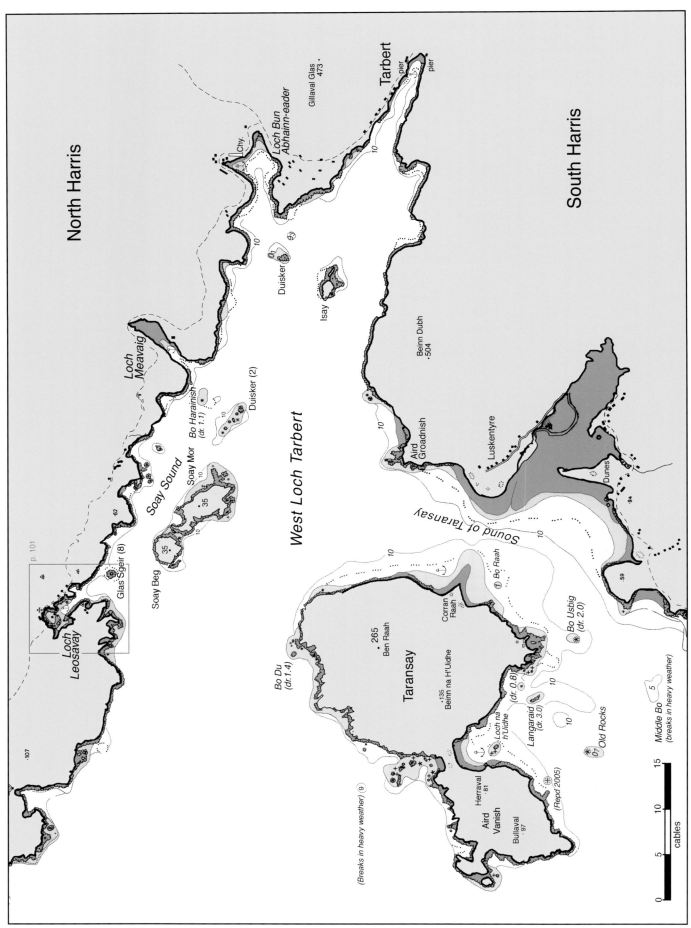

Taransay and West Loch Tarbert

West Loch Tarbert

Chart   (ii) 2841 Loch Maddy to Loch Resort including the Sound of Harris

Tide   Const. —0053 Ullapool (—0513 Dover) MHWS 4.2   MHWN 3.2   ML 2.3   MLWN 1.3   MLWS 0.4

Approach   **From the S** either side of Taransay may be taken, the W side being the cleaner. However if proceeding W about, keep 2 cables off the clearly seen offshore rocks on the W side and pass 3 cables off the N end of Taransay to avoid Bo Du (dr 1.4m) and associated reefs. If entering by the **Sound of Taransay**, Toe Head in line with the summit of Coppay astern bearing 245° clears Middle Bo to starboard and Bo Usbig (dr 2.0m) to port. Thereafter keep mid-channel to avoid the sandy spits on either side.

From the W enter S of the Taransay Glorigs avoiding Bo Molach 5 cables WSW of the Glorigs. Give the N point of Taransay a berth of 3 cables to avoid Bo Du (dr 1.4m). Further into the loch Isay can be passed on either hand to reach the head of the loch.

From the NW (see plan p. 102) Pass 1 mile W of Scarp to avoid the Obe Rocks and shallow 3m and 6m rocks further S before altering to pass N of the Old Rocks (dr. 0.3m and 2.3m) which lie 1 mile SW of Hushinish Point. Passing 5 cables off Hushinish Point on a course of 145° will leave the Hushinish Glorigs safely to port. The outermost Glorig is 12m high. Thereafter the approach to West Loch Tarbert is straightforward passing N of the Taransay Glorigs and giving the N point of Taransay a berth of 3 cables.

Anchorage **Tarbert** at the head of the loch S of the pier; well sheltered. Very heavy squalls from the S shore in strong S winds, when Loch Leosavay may be preferable. To Tarbert it is 18 miles from Leverburgh and about 11 miles from Toe Head. Facilities at East Loch Tarbert (see p. 74).

Loch Bun Abhainn-eader provides excellent shelter off the former whaling station identifiable by a conspic high brick chimney. In the approach Duisker, an above water rock with shoal rocks extending 2 cables N of it, can be avoided by keeping to either shore. Anchor SW of the ruined pier in the N arm. Other bays may also be suitable. Landing is difficult. Try the steps beside the steep slip at the former whaling station. Fish farm in the SE corner.

Loch Meavaig. Note Bo Harainish (dr. 1.1m) 2 cables SW of the entrance. Within the entrance there is deep water close inshore. Anchor off the house, about halfway up on the SE shore. The loch dries out 4 cables from the head. This anchorage is subject to SW'ly swell.

Taransay

Approach   **From the S** avoid Old Rocks (dr. 0.5m) 1 mile S of the entrance to Loch na h'Uidhe and also beware of the awash rock (Repd. 2005) 2.5c off the Aird Vanish shore and NNW of the Old Rocks. When entering the loch do not attempt to pass W of the drying rocks within the mouth of the bay. It is a little over 4 miles from Toe Head to Loch na h'Uidhe.

Anchorage **Loch na h'Uidhe.** Anchor either on the E or W side of the bay. Sheltered from the SW through N to SE. When leaving, or approaching from the N, note Langaraid (dr. 3.0m) and a rock (dr. 0.8m) 2 cables NE of it. If making for, or arriving from, West Loch Tarbert note the directions for avoiding Bo Usbig and the spits on either side of the channel off Corran Raah given above for the Sound of Taransay.

N of Corran Raah spit in 4m sand.

Loch Leosavay

Approach   Two cairns, one of which, high up on the hillside on the N side of the entrance, may help to identify the entrance to the loch from a distance. There are two further cairns, one on Glas Sgeir and another on the headland on the SW side of the entrance. Beware of the drying reef off this headland. **Note:** Glas Sgeir merges with the background rocks during the approach. The castle mansion on the N shore is conspic. when seen from a SE approach.

Anchorage The inner part of the loch on the W side opposite the stone quay on the N shore, is sheltered with good holding but beware of reported bottom chains. Use a strong tripping line. Note the drying rock off the stone quay. Alternatively anchor in the bay off the large mansion in 4m. There is an unmarked drying rock off the steps set into the sea wall at the head of the bay.

Hushinish Bay immediately E of Hushinish Point provides an attractive temporary anchorage in offshore winds.

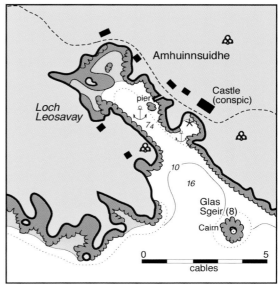

Loch Leosavay

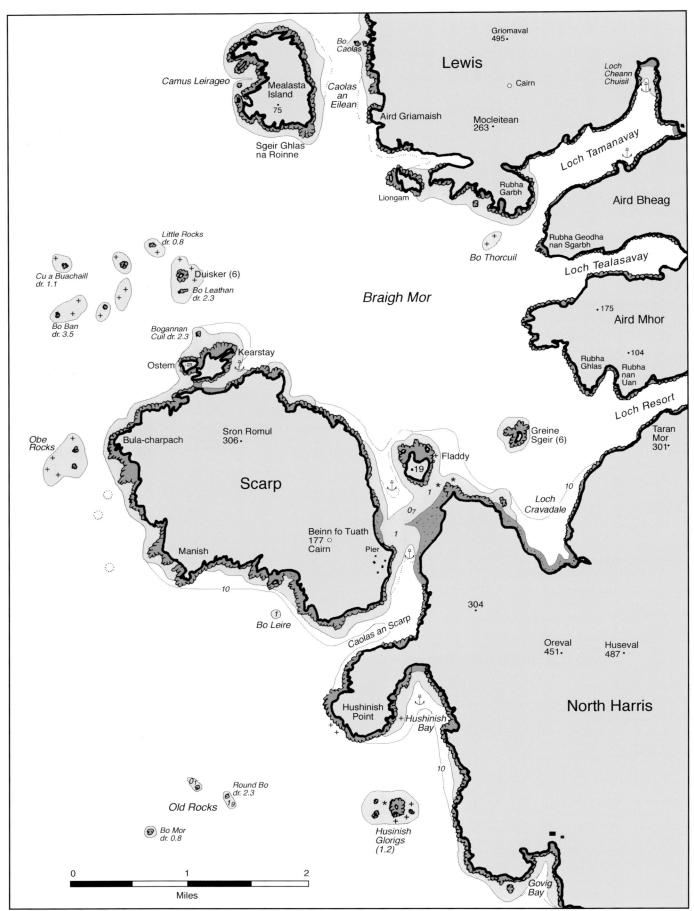

Griomaval
495 •

Lewis

Bo
Caolas

Loch
Cheann
Chuisil

Camus Leirageo

Mealasta
Island

Caolas
an
Eilean

○ Cairn

Aird Griamaish

Mocleitean
263 •

•75

Loch Tamanavay

Sgeir Ghlas
na Roinne

Liongam

Rubha
Garbh

Aird Bheag

Rubha Geodha
nan Sgarbh

Little Rocks
dr. 0.8

+ Bo Thorcuil

Loch Tealasavay

Cu a Buachaill
dr. 1.1

+ Duisker (6)

Braigh Mor

• 175

Aird Mhor

Bo Leathan
dr. 2.3

Bo Ban
dr. 3.5

• 104

Rubha
Ghlas

Rubha
nan
Uan

Bogannan
Cuil dr. 2.3

Kearstay

Loch Resort

Ostem

Greine
Sgeir (6)

Taran
Mor
301 •

Obe
Rocks

Sron Romul
306 •

• 19   + Fladdy

Bula-charpach

Scarp

1 * *

Loch
Cravadale

10

0 7

Beinn fo Tuath
177 ○
Cairn

1

Manish

Pier

304
•

10

Bo Leire

Caolas an Scarp

Oreval
451 •

Huseval
487 •

North Harris

Hushinish
Point

Hushinish
Bay

Old Rocks

Round Bo
dr. 2.3

19

Husinish
Glorigs
(1.2)

10

Bo Mor
dr. 0.8

Govig
Bay

0   1   2

Miles

Scarp, Loch Resort and Loch Tamanavay

Scarp

Chart (ii) 2841 Loch Maddy to Loch Resort including the Sound of Harris

General Lying 11 miles N of Toe Head at the entrance to the Sound of Harris, Scarp is separated from the mainland of North Harris by a shallow sound, Caolas an Scarp, which can be safely navigated under favourable weather and tidal conditions.

Tide Const. —0053 Ullapool (—0513 Dover) MHWS 4.2   MHWN 3.2   ML 2.3   MLWN 1.3   MLWS 0.4

Approach **From West Loch Tarbert** a passage N of Taransay Glorigs may be taken with care. The tangent of Hushinish Point under the right fall of the summit of Scarp clears these hazards and the Hushinish Glorigs. Passing 5 cables off Hushinish Point provides a sufficient safety margin to avoid the Old Rocks (dr. 0.2m and 2.3m) which lie 1 mile off Hushinish Point, the SW entrance to Caolas an Scarp. If continuing NW'wards keep at least 1 mile off Scarp and follow the directions for the approach to Scarp from the S in the following paragraph.

From the S aim to pass 1 mile E of Gasker Beg (10m) heading N. When abeam Gasker Beg alteration can be made towards Caolas an Scarp. Alternatively continue N'wards keeping at least a mile off Scarp to avoid off-lying rocks until it is possible to identify Bo Ban, the SW rock of the Duisker group of rocks lying NNW of Scarp, which is almost always marked by breakers. Keep Toe Head bearing not more than 167° till past W of all members of the Duisker group. When the S end of Mealasta Island bears 083° alter to that bearing until 5 cables from the island. If making for Loch Resort head mid-way between Greine Sgeir (6m) and Rubha Glas on the N side of the entrance. Passage S of the Duisker (6m) group, N of Scarp, should be undertaken only with very careful chart work using Chart 2841.

From the N the clearest approach is to pass 5 cables W of Mealasta. If making for Loch Resort head mid-way between Greine Sgeir (6m) and Rubha Glas, the N side of the entrance. The N approach may also be made through Caolas an Eilean between Mealasta Island and the Lewis shore. Tend to the island shore to avoid Bo Caolas lying 2 cables off the Lewis shore.

Caolas an Scarp

General Passage through this Sound is straightforward provided it is not attempted before half tide as the depth over the bar can be less than 1 metre at LWS, but see Caution below. An extensive sandy spit extends for 3 cables off the Harris shore where the bar is shallowest N of the houses and pier on Scarp. Accordingly hold to the Scarp shore when proceeding either N or S. **Caution**. If there is a N'ly swell a passage through Caolas an Scarp could be dangerous.

Tide Const. —0053 Ullapool (—0513 Dover) MHWS 4.2   MHWN 3.2   ML 2.3   MLWN 1.3   MLWS 0.4
In Caolas an Scarp the streams run as follows
N-going stream begins —0420 Ullapool (+0345 Dover)
S-going stream begins +0205 Ullapool (—0215 Dover)
Although the Admiralty Pilot refers to the tidal streams being barely perceptible, a southerly current of 2 knots has been experienced and a similar rate north-going may be expected.

Anchorage There are suitable anchorage depths at the **N and S sides of the bar** in Caolas an Scarp but both locations are likely to be affected by the tidal streams.

Kearstay The sound between this small island and the N shore of Scarp provides good shelter from the S and NW in attractive surroundings. Enter from the NE. The W entrance is impassable. The sandy beach is quite steep and prone to surf. (see photograph p. 99)

Loch Resort

General This loch is well protected from the W as it lies due E of Scarp. The approach is straightforward passing N of Greine Sgeir. Anchor off the mouth of a burn at the widest part of the loch on the S side 2.5 miles from the entrance. Ensure that the anchor is well bedded in. Some boulders close inshore cover at HW. There are fierce squalls in strong winds. In such winds the sea state off Taran Mor, a spectacular cliff within the entrance, is very violent.

Loch Tamanavay.

Approach Keep close to the N or preferably the E shore at the mouth of the loch to avoid the Bo Thorcuil Rocks off the middle of the entrance. The NE side of Mealasta Island open of Liongam on a bearing of 330° leads SW of Bo Thorcuil. Do not rely on the sea breaking over these rocks to identify their presence.

Anchorage There is good shelter at the head of the loch but note that depths decrease rather sharply. The bay on the S side, E of a promontory, is reported foul with lost moorings.

Camas Uig

Anchorage Less than 2M NE of Ard More Mangersta this wide bay provides good anchorage but it is dangerously exposed in NW winds. (See chart 2515 Ard More Mangersta to Tiumpan Head)

West Loch Roag

Chart (iii) 2515 covers both West and East Loch Roag

General As will be seen from Chart 2515 there are numerous opportunities for exercising pilotage skills in this very attractive loch and many anchorages, often close by sandy beaches, will be found. The following paragraphs are merely an introduction to the area. It should be noted that, although getting to Loch Roag by sea may be a time-consuming challenge, there are excellent bus services to Stornoway where ferry and air services can facilitate crew changes.

Tide Const. —0026 Ullapool (—0446 Dover) MHWS 4.2 MHWN 3.2 ML 2.3 MLWN 1.3 MLWS 0.4

Approach The entrance to West Loch Roag is between Gallan Head to the W and Old Hill (92m), an island shaped like a loaf of bread, to the N. After giving Gallan Head a berth of 5 cables to avoid Sgeir Gallan (dr 3.4m), steer to pass mid-way between Pabay Beag and Harsgeir. If intending to proceed into the upper reaches of the loch pass 0.5 mile NE of Pabay Mor and Vacsay and bring the E side of Vacsay to bear 193°. Then head to pass mid-way between Geile Sgeir and Rubha Rollinish, passing W of Bogha Bhad Ghlais (dr 2.4m) and E of Bogha na Muilne (dr 0.9m) which lies 1 cable E of Eilean Teinish in the Sound of Vuia. Note the clearance bearings given on Chart 2515.

Pabay Mor

Anchorage **On the E side** of Pabay Mor in the bay off **Traigh na Cille** lying N of Sgeir na Cille (9m). This anchorage is identified by a sandy beach, the only one on the E side of Pabay Mor. Approach the entrance from the NNE holding to the E shore. Anchor in 2 to 4m sand.

Alternatively anchor off the SE side of **Sgeir na Cille.** When passing through Caolas na Sgeire Leithe, keep at least 1 cable off the outermost islet, Sgeir na Chaorach h-Aon to avoid Bogha Bhealt (dr 2.4m). Anchor off the cave, 5m, in sand. (See plan)

Valtos

Anchorage In the approach through the sound between Pabay and Vacsay keep in mid-channel but when turning to starboard note the shoal water S of Pabay Mor and Three Hook Rock, a submerged rock 2 cables SE of the SE corner of Pabay Mor. **Anchor off the NW or SE sides of Shiaram Mor** in 3 to 4m sand. Valtos Pier dries and it should not be approached without local knowledge.

Eilean Teinish,

Anchorage Safe anchorage in all summer weather can be found in the **Sound of Vuia inside Eilean Teinish**. Note Bogha na Muilne (dr 0.9m) 1 cable NE of Eilean Teinish. The S approach to the anchorage is straightforward but beware of an extensive mussel farm less than a cable to the SE of the anchorage. Easy access to the superb Traigh na Berie to the N.

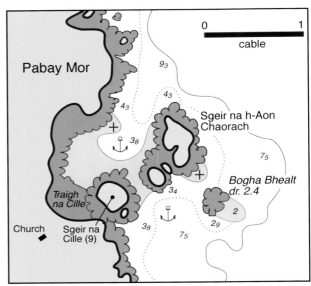
Pabay Mor

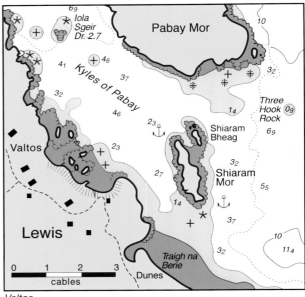
Valtos

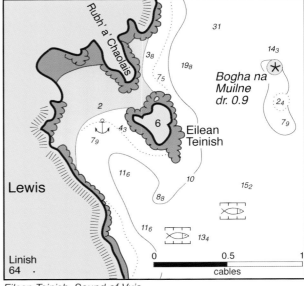
Eilean Teinish, Sound of Vuia

Miavaig pontoon   *Randal Coe*

Loch Miavaig

General   The outer approach through Miavaig Bay is encumbered with fish farms. The narrow entrance to the loch leads to a wider area for anchoring. There is now the facility of a pontoon with water and electricity.

Facilities   At Miavaig. Diesel (key card needed, see p.5). and calor gas. Shop, P.O. and garage at Timsgarry 2.5 miles away by road. Local shop owner (tel. 01851 672285) will help with deliveries.

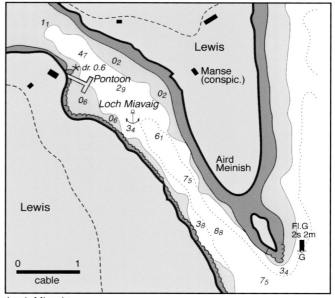

Loch Miavaig

Looking East from Valtos over West Loch Roag   *Hugh Henderson*

East Loch Roag

Chart   (iii) 2515 covers East and West Loch Roag.

General   The general comments made in regard to West Loch Roag about pilotage opportunities apply also to East Loch Roag.

Tide   Const. —0020 Ullapool (—0440 Dover) MHWS 4.2   MHWN 3.2   ML 2.3   MLWN 1.3   MLWS 0.4

Lights   Aird Laimishader   Fl 6s 63m 8M   Wh framework Twr
Greinam   Fl WR 6s 8m 8/7M   Wh beacon

Approach   The W side of the entrance is identified by Old Hill (92m), an island shaped like a loaf of bread, and the E side by Aird Laimishader with its conspic. Lt tower. Approaching from the W yachts can pass between Cul Campay (12m) and Sgeir Dhearg (2m) which is SE of Mas Sgeir, but the bottom is uneven so that the seas have a greater tendency to break. It is better in such conditions to pass N of Mas Sgeir. Thereafter maintain a course in the centre of the loch.

At Night East Loch Roag is the only anchorage on the W side of the Outer Hebrides which may be approached at night with the aid of the lights noted above. The red sector of Greinam Light between bearings 143° and 169° covers the dangers on the NE side of East Loch Roag. Fish farms NW and SE of Greinam could be a hazard at night.

Anchorage   **Port a' Chaoil** 3 miles S of Loch Carloway is sheltered from most weather. Note Sgeir nan Sgarbh (dr 1.9m), not named on Chart 2515, which lies at the SW side of the entrance to the bay and rocks in the middle of the head of the bay. 3m is found well offshore. To go further in, keep to the E side to avoid rocks.

Breasclete Bay. Anchor E of the substantial new pier showing FR (vert) and just S of the old pier in 4m. The new pier has berths for off-loading fish and supplying fishing vessels; depth 2.9m alongside at MLWS. **Facilities:** Shop 200m left at crossroads. Petrol on right at crossroads. Water at new pier.

Callanish. Temporary anchorage to visit the **Standing Stones** and Visitors Centre. Anchor NW of **Bratanish Mor** in 2m to 3m. **Facilities:** Shop at Callanish. Restaurant at Garynahine 1M.

Caution Note the overhead electric cable 3.8m above HWS crosses the mouth of Loch Ceann Hulavig.

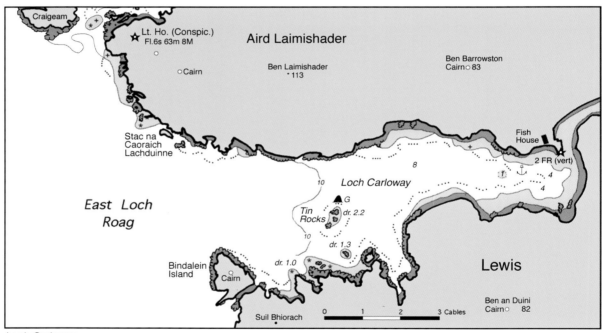

Loch Carloway

Loch Carloway

Approach   In the approach the Tin Rocks (dr. 2.2m) in the middle of the loch are marked by a G con buoy. There is also a shoal patch with at least depth 1.0m in mid-loch SW of the pier.

Anchorage   Off Carloway Pier (2FR vert) at the head of the loch in 3 to 4m. There is 0.3m alongside the pier, and small craft may find shelter E of it.

Facilities   Stores, P.O., Water at pier. Diesel (key card needed, see p.5). Petrol 1.5 miles on the Stornoway road.

Interest   Dun Carloway, one of the most complete Pictish Brochs in the British Isles, is 0.5 mile from the S shore.

Kirkibost

General The very well sheltered basin of Dubh Thob lies on the W side of East Loch Roag between Great Bernera and Vacasay Island. It is better known as Kirkibost. By arrangement a yacht might be left here in safety.

Lights Entrance channel lights;
W side: FL G 3s 2M Grey post on the Great Bernera shore.
E side: Fl R 3s 2M Metal column on the tidal rock off Vacasay Island.
Kirkibost Pier lights: 2FG (vert) 2M

Approach From the N pass mid-channel between the entrance light beacons.

Anchorage Kirkibost pier is on the W side of the basin. A line of drying rocks extends from the S shore to a red beacon half a cable E of the pier head. Anchor in 3m. There is 1.8m alongside the pier.

Facilities Diesel (key card needed, see p.5). and water by hose at pier. Showers at Community Centre.

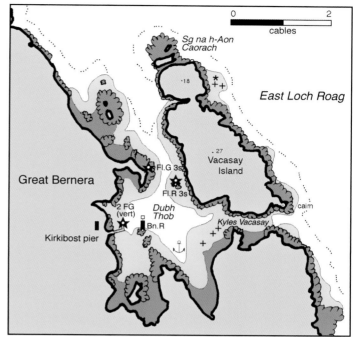

Kirkibost (Dubh Thob)

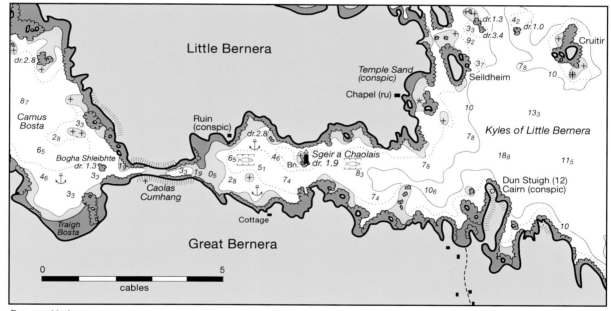

Bernera Harbour

Bernera Harbour

General This very sheltered anchorage lies between Little and Great Bernera but is somewhat obstructed by fish farms.

Approach Pass 1 cable E and S of Cruitir which is 3 cables E of Little Bernera, and then pass half a cable S of the SE point of Little Bernera. To avoid rocks extending from the S shore do not stray S of a line joining Dun Stuigh (12m), marked by a cairn, at the S side of the entrance, and Sgeir a' Chaolais (dr 1.9m) marked with a beacon (BW cage on pole) situated well within the harbour. Pass S of Sgeir a'Chaolais.

Anchorage Anchor **WNW of Sgeir a'Chaolais** avoiding a rock (dr 2.8m) close to the NE shore and a submerged rock 1 cable SE of the ruin if using the **S anchorage.**

The narrow passage to the W through Caolas Cumhang to Camas Bosta has 0.6m at LWS and can be negotiated with great care above half tide when the depth is over 2m. Local knowledge is essential. The rock (dr 1.3m) at the W entrance to the narrows should be passed on its S side.

Camas Bosta on the W side of the narrows is a fine summer anchorage. Good holding in sand. The approach from W Loch Roag demands special care. There is a restored Iron Age House on shore.

Loch Roag to the Butt of Lewis

Charts
(i) 2721 St Kilda to the Butt of Lewis
(iii) 2515 Ard More Mangersta to Tiumpan including Loch Roag

General
From Gallan Head to the Butt of Lewis is about 30 miles. N of the entrances to West and East Loch Roag the coastline is much less mountainous than further S. From Tiumpan, 1 mile NE of the entrance to East Loch Roag, to the Butt of Lewis it is 21 miles along an exposed coast which provides only a degree of shelter in off shore winds. For example in the bay N of the Dell Rock (8) which lies 2.5M from the SW extremity of the Butt, an approach towards the Church and houses on shore will find depths suitable for anchoring. The bottom is reported as sand.

Tides
Across the entrances to West and East Loch Roag the streams run NE and SW.
The spring rate in each direction is less than 1knot
NE-going stream begins —0420 Ullapool (+0345 Dover)
SW-going stream begins +0205 Ullapool (—0215 Dover)

Off the NW coast of Lewis the rate of the tide off salient points can be up to 2kn, but less between the points and offshore.

Lights and marks

Flannan Isles	Fl (2) 30s 101m 20M	Wh Twr on Eilean Mor
Aird Laimishader	Fl 6s 63m 8M	Wh framework Twr
(N point of East Loch Roag)		
Butt of Lewis LH	Fl 5s 52m 25M	Red brick twr

Radio Masts on Ard More Mangersta (4 M south of Gallan Head)
Radio Masts at the Butt of Lewis

Force 2/3 at the Butt of Lewis   *Jane Routh*

Rounding the Butt of Lewis

Charts
(i) 2721 St Kilda to the Butt of Lewis
(ii) 1785 The North Minch - Northern Part

General
The rounding of the Butt of Lewis is considered to be more dangerous than rounding Cape Wrath due to the tidal conditions mentioned below and the ever present swell which is often from different directions. **In no circumstances should the Butt of Lewis be approached when white water is seen off it.**

Tide
Around the Butt of Lewis the NE-going stream W of the point, and the E and SE-going streams E of the point, start almost simultaneously as do the streams when they are going N, W and SW. The commencement of these are as follows:–

NE, E and SE streams begin —0445 Ullapool (+0320 Dover)
N,W and SW-going streams begin +0140 Ullapool (—0150 Dover)

The rate at springs is 4–5kn in both directions close to the point and 3kn a mile offshore. However there can be severe turbulence beyond that distance and the point should be given a berth of at least 5 miles, except in settled conditions. **Note**: During the W-going stream an eddy sets NE along the coast from a several miles SW of the Butt of Lewis. Similarly during the SE-going stream an eddy runs N along the E coast of Lewis from Rubha Geal to the Butt of Lewis. Violent turbulence can be expected where the eddies meet the main streams.

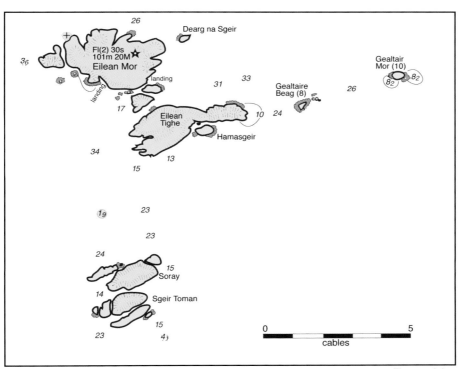

Flannan Isles

Flannan Isles

Charts   (i) 2721 St Kilda to Butt of Lewis
             (i) 2720 Flannan Isles to Sule Skerry
             (iii) 2524 Islands off the North West Coast of Scotland
             OS 13

General   The main group of islands comprise Eilean Mor with lighthouse on the summit, and Eilean Tighe. Two islets, Gealtaire Beag (8) and Gealtaire Mor (10) lie about half a mile E of Eilean Tighe. There are two other groups of smaller islands, the Soray group being half a mile S, and the other 2 miles W comprising Roareim and Eilean a' Ghobha. The only island upon which it is feasible to land on is Eilean Mor.

Light   Eilean Mor Lt Ho.   Fl.(2) 30s 101m 20M   Wh twr

Tide   Const. —0031 Ullapool (—0451 Dover) MHWS 3.9   MHWN 3.0   ML 1.7   MLWN 1.4   MLWS 0.5

Anchorage   **Temporary anchorage** can be found either E or W of the islet between Eilean Mor and Eilean Tighe. A swell is normally present. There are steps and mooring rings on the E side of Eilean Mor (N of the islet) and also on the S side. None of these are now maintained and they may be in a dangerous and unusable state. The NLB can accept no responsibility for unauthorised mooring or landing. The shores of Eilean Mor and Eilean Tighe are steep to without hidden dangers except as shown on the plan. Anchoring in 7m close to Eilean Mor is possible, or in deeper water further off. A tripping line should be used as the bottom is rock.

Flannan Isles looking SE from Eilean Mor Light House   *Charles Tait*

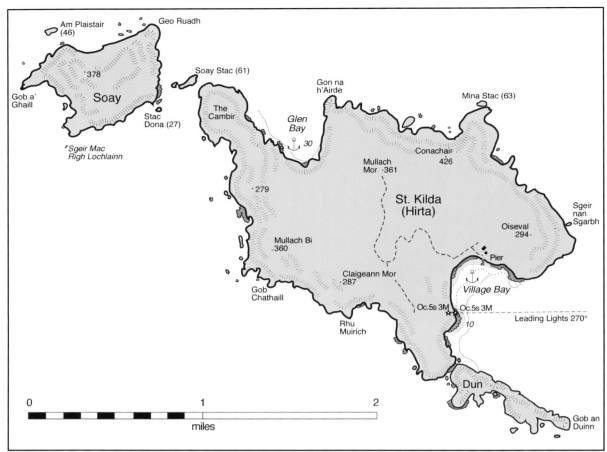

St. Kilda

St Kilda

Charts
(i)   2721 St Kilda to Butt of Lewis
(i)   2722 Skerryvore to St. Kilda
(iii) 2524 Islands off the North West Coast of Scotland
OS18

General
The St Kilda Group consists of four islands, St Kilda (otherwise named Hirta), Dun, Soay and Boreray. There are three significant stacks; Levenish just over a mile E from the extremity of Dun, and Stac Lee and Stac an Armin each about 2 cables W and N of Boreray respectively.

The St Kilda group of islands and stacks is a World Heritage site and National Nature Reserve. The group is owned by the National Trust for Scotland. The management of the island of St Kilda is in the hands of the Ranger to whom all visitors to the island should report upon arrival. When intending to visit it is helpful if contact is made with the National Trust Western Isles Manager. (tel: 01463 232034)

Lights
Leading lights on cairns bearing 270° on W side of Village Bay
Front: Oc 5s 26m 3M   Rear: Oc 5s 38m 3M

Mark
Flag pole beside pier on E side of Village Bay

Caution
There is a good element of risk in going out to St Kilda as changes in weather are sometimes sudden.

Passage
It is 42 miles from Pabbay on the W side of the Sound of Harris to St Kilda. If the visibility is good the group comes into view when about half way across, shaped like a full rigged sailing ship, but, when nearer, the islands and stacks are seen separately. Should the weather deteriorate when either on passage to or leaving from St Kilda, and the options of returning to the Sound of Harris or seeking shelter in Loch Resort are decided against, the likelihood is that the best choice will be to make for Loch Roag (see pp. 104-107).

Tides
Const. —0055 Ullapool (—0515 Dover) MHWS 3.3   MHWN 2.5   ML 1.8   MLWN 1.2   MLWS 0.4
NE-going stream begins +0545 Ullapool (+0125 Dover)
SW-going stream begins —0030 Ullapool (—0450 Dover)
Close to the islands in the group the spring rate is 3kn.

Village Bay, St Kilda   *Charles Tait*

St Kilda (continued)

Approach   In the approach to Village Bay note the position of Levenish (55) the stack lying 1.5 miles E of Dun, which has a ridge of rock, Na Bodham drying 1.5m close-in on E side, and shoal water extending W for 4 cables. Between Levenish and the SE end of Dun there are overfalls with wind against tide (3 knots at springs). These overfalls extend across the the channel between Dun and Levenish. Village Bay which faces SE is sheltered on the W side by Dun and is free from hidden dangers although on occasions a strong tide rip sets across the mile wide mouth of the bay. If approaching W-about round the island of Soay beware of the tide race with a N-going tide off the NW side of Soay.

Anchorage   **Village Bay.** Although a full Atlantic swell sets into the bay there is reasonable shelter in 5-6m off the pier below the Church. Good holding in hard sand. However it is essential to clear out should the wind come from between E and S. In such conditions a lee can be had anywhere off the shores round the island which are clear outside one cable but there is nowhere to anchor except in **Glen Bay on the N** side. There it is possible to anchor within a stone's throw of the beach, but a little further out it deepens from 13m to 30m. The bottom is rocky and the anchor must be buoyed. This anchorage must be vacated if there is any tendency for the wind to go N of W.

Landing   There is always some swell in Village Bay unless there has been a prolonged period of calm. It is advisable not to delay going ashore to visit the island as it may be necessary to clear out at short notice should a serious swell develop. To land make for the W side of the pier and if necessary move to the root of the pier where there is a small cove with shelving sand. The Ranger must be contacted by all visitors to the island. No dogs are allowed ashore.

Facilities   Shop for tourist souvenirs only. Water at tap near pier.

Interest   The Ranger and representatives of the National Trust of Scotland will be pleased to provide information on all aspects of the history of St Kilda. The web site *www.kilda.org.uk* is certainly worth consulting when planning a visit.

Gaelic for yachtsmen

An ability to interpret the commoner Gaelic place names can be not only a source of interest to the yachtsman but a real aid to navigation. Many obscure and romantic looking names are in fact simple descriptions of the physical appearance of landmarks such as black rock, grey point, etc. Spelling and pronunciation are difficulties which cannot be fully explained in a single page but the following observations may be helpful. Gaelic is an ancient tongue with words borrowed from many source languages and until modern times was seldom written down, so that spelling is largely the result of scholars attempting to record the spoken word in all its forms. The form of words varies according to gender, number, case etc. and it is not always obvious that several apparently different words are actually forms of the same word, e.g. muir, mara, mhara and marannan. The insertion of the letter `h' apparently at random can alter the appearance and pronunciation of a word, e.g. mor and mhor.

In addition, the original Gaelic form is often anglicised into a more genteel form, e.g. coire becomes corry. The compilers of charts, maps, pilot books and sailing directions have not adopted any consistent scheme of spelling with the result that the same place name can appear in several different forms. Pronunciation is so difficult that the yachtsman is referred to a grammar or dictionary but one rule will help greatly. There is no `v' in written Gaelic so `bh' and `mh' are both pronounced as `v', e.g. bhan sounds van and mhor sounds vore. The following glossary is arranged in groups which it is hoped will help the navigator to identify what he is looking at and which can be easily learned by heart and thus constantly be at the yachtsman's service.

Glossary

Colours

dubh, dhubh, dubha, dow	black
geal, gheal, geala	white
ban, bhan, bana	fair
breac, bhreac, breaca	speckled
buidhe, bowie, buie, vuie	yellow
dearg, deirge	red
donn	brown
garbh, garbha, gharbh, garve	rough
glas, ghlas, glasa	grey (or green)
gorm, ghorm, gorma	blue
liath, leithe	grey
odhar, uidhre	dun coloured
ruadh, ruadha	red
uaine	green

Size & Shape

mor, mhor, mhoir, more	large
beag, bheag, bhig, beaga	small
fada	long
ord, uird	round
leathan	broad

Physical features

abhainn, avon, alit, auld	river, burn
acairseid	anchorage
achadh, ach, auch	field
ailean, aline	plain
ard, aird	promontory
bàgh	bay
beinn, ben	mountain
bo, bogha	sunk rock
bruach	bank, precipice
bun, bon	root, mouth of a river
caladh	harbour
camus, camas	bay
caol, caolas, kyle	narrows
clach, clachan, cloiche	stone, house, village
cladach	shore, beach
coir, coire, corry	hollow, whirlpool
creag, creige, craig, crag	rock, cliff
cnoc, knock	knoll, round hill
dun, duin	fortress
eilean, eileanan (plural)	island
fasgadh	shelter
muir, mara, mhara, marannan	sea
poll, puill	pool
rubha, rhu	point of land
sgeir	above water rock
sruth	current
traigh	shore, sand-beach
uamh	cave

Parts of the body

beul, beoil, bheoil	mouth
cas	foot
ceann, kin, ken, cinn	head
druim	back
fiacal, fiacaill	tooth
sron, sroine	nose

Animals, Birds and Fish

bo, ba	cow
breck, breac, bhric, brice	trout
caora, caorach	sheep
dobhran	otter
each, eck, eich	horse
gamhna	stirk
gobhar, gabhar, goibhre	goat
iolaire	eagle
ron, roin	seal
tarbh	bull

People

balach	boy
ban-righ	queen
bean, mna, mnathe	wife
bodach	old man
buachaille	shepherd
caileag	girl
cailleach	old woman
fear, fir, (duine, daoine)	man
gille, gillean	boy
iasgair	fisherman
righ	king

Directions

tuath	north
deas	south
ear	east
iar	west

Trees & plants

beith	birch
call, coil	hazel
craobh, craoibhe	tree
darach, darroch	oak
fraoch, fraoich	heather

Buildings

aros	house
baile, bhaile	town
caisteal	castle
cille, kil, sill, ceall	church
clachan	village
dun	fort
tigh	house
tobar, tober, tobair	well

Submarine Exercise Areas

Keep the echo sounder running if passing through an exercise area when submarines are operating. Warnings of areas allocated for exercises are given by Stornoway Coastguard after the weather forecast at 0710 and 1910. Clyde Coastguard broadcasts the warnings at 0810 and 2010.

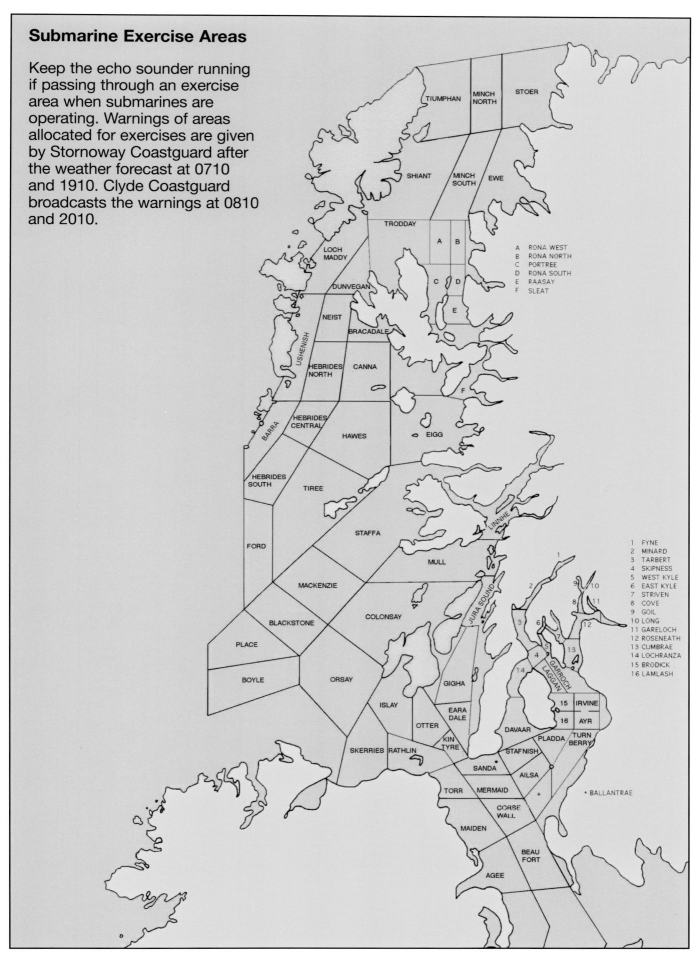

A   RONA WEST
B   RONA NORTH
C   PORTREE
D   RONA SOUTH
E   RAASAY
F   SLEAT

1   FYNE
2   MINARD
3   TARBERT
4   SKIPNESS
5   WEST KYLE
6   EAST KYLE
7   STRIVEN
8   COVE
9   GOIL
10 LONG
11 GARELOCH
12 ROSENEATH
13 CUMBRAE
14 LOCHRANZA
15 BRODICK
16 LAMLASH

THE CLYDE CRUISING CLUB

The Clyde Cruising Club was formed in 1909 with the object of encouraging cruising, cruising races, and fostering the social side of sailing. These activities are still the mainstay of the Club with cruising musters and cruises in company being held at various venues on the West Coast and further afield. Additionally the Club organises a full programme of offshore and inshore races throughout the season including the well known Tobermory race and the Scottish Series on Loch Fyne which has developed into one of the biggest yachting events in Britain.

An important part of the Club's present activities is the training and encouragement of young sailors, including especially children and young adults who are disabled, at the Club's new premises on Bardowie Loch.

The Club is also represented on many national and local organisations and is regularly consulted on matters of concern to all cruising yachtsmen: moorings, fish farms, buoyage, weather forecasts and similar topics. Anyone interested in joining the Club, taking part in any of the above activities and lending their support to the voice of the Club is warmly invited to email or write to the Secretary at the address below.

An incidental but worthwhile benefit of membership is entitlement to a very generous discount on the purchase of Sailing Directions !

Sailing Directions for Scottish Waters have been produced by the Club for more than ninety years and over this time they have become widely recognised as valuable and authoritative pilotage guides. They are published in six volumes which are regularly updated with the latest information on approximately an annual basis. The books currently published by CCC Publications are listed below and can be obtained from any good chandler or direct from the Club office.

1. **The Firth of Clyde**
   (inc. the North Channel, the Solway Firth and Isle of Man)

2. **Kintyre to Ardnamurchan**

3. **Ardnamurchan to Cape Wrath**

4. **Outer Hebrides**

5. **North & North East Scotland and Orkney Islands**

6. **Shetland Islands**

Clyde Cruising Club
Suite 101, The Pentagon Centre
35 Washington Street
Glasgow G3 8AZ Scotland
Tel: 0141 221 2774 email: hazel@clyde.org, www.clyde.org